What Teens
Need Most
from Their
Parents

Other Books by Bill Sanders

Tough Turf
Outtakes: Devotions for Girls
Outtakes: Devotions for Guys
Goalposts: Devotions for Girls
Goalposts: Devotions for Guys
Life, Sex, and Everything in Between
What Your Kids Are Up To and In For

What Teens Need Most from Their Parents

Bill Sanders

© 1987 by Bill Sanders

Published by Fleming H. Revell
a division of Baker Book House Company
P.O. Box 6287, Grand Rapids, MI 49516-6287

Spire edition published 1997

Previously published under the title *Almost Everything Teens Want Parents to Know: But Are Afraid to Tell Them*

Printed in the United States of America

ISBN 0-8007-8641-6

Scripture taken from the King James Version of the Bible.

Acknowledgments

Special thanks to my dad and mom, John and Lorie Sanders, for being the greatest parents in the world. They gave all six of us quality *and* quantity time, along with every ounce of love in their hearts.

Next, to my wife, Holly, who believed I could complete this book and continually said so. My daughter Emily even stayed quiet many hours so her daddy could write "that lousy book."

Kathy Reisner, my faithful and talented office manager, typed and edited many pages over and over, with support and belief in the entire project.

Cheryl Garlock got her typewriter out after Kathy was gone this summer and worked hard to help me make the deadline.

Thanks also to the hundreds of teens and parents and friends who shared practical parenting tips that have made this book so useful for teens' parents.

Most of all I want to thank God for giving me the opportunity and for linking me up with Fleming H. Revell and Pamela Landfear, who has put her magical editing touch on my efforts to better equip you, the reader, to reach your teen.

Contents

Preface

Every year I speak to thousands of teens—sometimes more than 10,000 in one week. After I've talked to them, at least one comes up to me and says, "When you talk to my parents, in their session tonight, tell them. . . ." "Don't forget to share with them that. . . ." "Whatever you do, please mention this for me. . . ." "Don't tell them who I am, just tell them this. They need to know!"

In a time when parenting seems to be one of the hardest things to do and when parents seem to have difficulty getting through to their young people, I keep hearing that kids really *do* want to get close to mom and dad—and I hear it from the teens themselves.

So often I get letters and comments from teens that reflect that desire, but also show that sons and daughters wish they knew how to get through to their parents.

They'll tell me things like this:

Dear Mr. Sanders:

I heard your speech at our school. You really got to me. I laughed more in that one hour than I had in a long, long time. Though I tried to get my parents to come and listen to you at the evening session, they wouldn't.

I have a problem I have to tell you about; you're the only one who will listen. [Many times I've never met the student, but he or she has been to hear me speak and feels confident I will listen and write back.]

No matter what I do, I can't please my parents. Sometimes I feel they actually hate me. They don't say it, but they sure do act it. We always argue and fight, and life just isn't worth living. What should I do? I've read your book for teens, *Tough Turf*, but I still don't know how to please my parents.

Please write.

Sincerely,
A Hurting Teen

After my session, when they come to ask me questions, one on one or in a group, teens tell me how they feel about their parents—what they wish they'd do or not do. As they share their individual situations, I try to give them some help that will bring them closer to mom and dad.

At night, when I speak to parents, I share the tips I've heard from teens and try to remind them what it was like to be a teen. I also give them ideas I know work with teens, because I've seen it happen.

Maybe teens would not phrase each concern exactly the way I have here, but they all have the needs I've addressed—needs only a parent can fill. In fact, I've based this book primarily on two sets of experts—teens and parents with young-adult children (they have gotten through those tough teen years).

I've tried to fill this volume with lots of specific, practical, how-to ideas your whole family can start using today. All nineteen chapters may not fit you, but don't stop on the first, if it's not what you need. Keep going until you find the ideas that can help you build a better family.

However, just reading this book won't solve all your problems. You also need to put the ideas into practice—have a change in behavior in your family, your teen, you, and your spouse. If you don't do some things differently after you've read it, you've missed out on the purpose of this book: for you to live in a way more pleasing to yourselves, your Maker, and the world around you.

Give it a try. I know you can do it!

Introduction:
One Standard Size

On a typical day, in a typical school, my first assembly starts at 8:30. It takes the students (all 900 of them) about ten minutes to file into the auditorium. After my introduction, I stand in front of them for an hour and do my thing: I try to make them *laugh* and *cry* and *think*. Most of all I try to make them realize that life is worth living and they can develop the resources necessary to handle any problems that are ever thrown at them.

I tell them how as a kid I was skinny and had a big nose, that I couldn't find out what it took to be popular, that I had dealings with drugs that caused me not to be able to have children, and I share my own personal and social problems, to show them I'm human. Once they start laughing and unfolding their arms, I begin to share the real message: how to say *yes* to themselves, the people around them, to their Maker, and to America. I also show them ways to say no with dignity to drugs, the wrong influences,

13

and to people, places, things, or activities that could ruin their futures.

Once I've done these things, I see a student body do some things many people never witness in an entire lifetime: These teens applaud the putdown of alcohol, drugs, making fun of other people—and applaud the idea that you should be a virgin when you marry.

After the assembly, young people stand up, come to me, and hand me their cigarettes, saying, "I'm stopping today because of you." Or I hear them say, "You wouldn't believe all the kids who are throwing their drugs down the drain in the bathroom." Some come to me and comment, "You really know how to relate to us. Thanks for caring." Then they ask, "Can I write to you? Can you help me? Can I talk to you for a while? I have nothing to live for, and I need someone who will listen."

I hold many of them in my arms. We cry together, and I rarely leave without giving away at least one handkerchief. While they talk, I listen, and they share their hurts, pains, and concerns with a person they trust—someone they probably never will see again. As they open up to me, they explain how they have *no one* else to turn to: not mom or dad, a friend or teacher. In their climb for success and recognition, they feel they've entered a dark, scary world, and that the stairs have started crashing beneath them.

Are these just the "losers" of the class? No. I talk to the 200-pound jocks, the president of the junior class, the captain of the cheerleading squad, the heavy-set girl, and the pimply-faced sophomore. Though they come in all heights, widths, and designs, their hurts and problems come in one standard size— GIGANTIC!

One evening before a parents' session, in a five-minute conversation with a senior girl, I learned a lifelong lesson. When she shared how worthless life had become since her boyfriend had broken up with her, I replied, "That's not the worst thing in the world." With desperation written on every inch of her face, she said, "*It is to me!*" Then and there I learned the importance of taking young people at their word and not making a judgment about the size of another's shoes, when I can't walk in them.

That's one thing I try to share when I speak to parents: I try to have them walk in their teen's shoes for a while and to see how much alike parents and teens really are. I also try to make them see that things can change, no matter how bad things may seem in their family.

Look to the Future

When—usually at the urging of their young people—mom and dad come to the evening sessions I hold, I begin with a few questions. "How many of you think people are improvable?" I ask, and their hands raise. "How many of you are fairly sure you are people?" I can read their thoughts in their eyes: *That's a trick question, right?* But slowly their hands go up.

"How many of you are married?" I query. Most put up a hand. "How many of you would like to be married next year?" Again they wonder if it's a trick question, but their hands raise, some quite slowly as husband and wife look at each other for reassurance. Then I ask, "To the same person?" At that they begin to laugh, to realize that it's okay to have a good time here.

Next we play "Let's Pretend," in which I ask them to imagine that we have two large boxes in the front of the auditorium. In the first they place their car keys, new house, the place on the lake, their boat, new stereo, video equipment, wardrobe, talents, hopes, dreams, accomplishments—everything they're most proud of. The second box contains something more important than fifty of those boxes put together: our young people, the future of America—its only future. What we invest in them will truly count for a long, long time.

Investing in our children doesn't only mean the ones we raise, though. When my kid hurts, it's the same as if yours did. If you see my four-year-old daughter standing in the road as a car zooms down it, I hope you'll run just as fast to save her as you would for your own son. Believe me, I'd do it if I saw your kid standing there. If your son just got arrested for drug trafficking, I'd hurt as if he were mine, because in the same neighborhood, in the same circumstances, he *might* be mine.

I also realize many parents take the place of *both* mom and dad, because of a divorce or death in the family. In many communities, more than half are single-parent homes. These people do the toughest job in the world: the job of two done by one. Single mom or dad, the rest of us in the community need to ask your forgiveness, because we haven't always given you the patience or support you've needed, and we need your help, patience, and prayers, because we're all in this together. Whether I say "mom and dad" or "parents" I mean all of us.

Listen to Your Teens

Our kids need to become winners, and we have the biggest influence on their lives. But if we don't hear the words they say and the subtle messages that give hints of what they wish they *could* say, we might not have any influence at all.

One teen sent me this poem, that explains it all:

PLEASE!!
Please hear what I am not saying.
Don't be fooled by me.

Don't be fooled by the face I wear.
For I wear a thousand masks, masks
That I am afraid to take off . . .
And none of them are me.
Pretending is an art that is second
Nature with me but don't be fooled.
I give the impression that I am secure,
That all is sunny and unruffled with me,
That confidence is my name
And coolness is my game,
That the water is calm and I am in command,
And that I need no one.
Please don't believe me. Please.

My surface may seem smooth,
But my surface is my mask.
Beneath this lies no complacence.
Beneath dwells the real me,
In confusion, in fear, and aloneness.
But I hide this. I don't want anyone to know it.
I panic at the thought of my weakness
And I fear of being exposed.
That's why I frantically create a mask to hide
*   behind.*
A nonchalant, sophisticated facade,
To help me pretend,
To shield me from the glance that knows.
But such a glance is precisely my salvation.
My only salvation and I know it.
That is, if it is followed by acceptance,
If it is followed by love.

It is the only thing that will assure me,
Of what I can't assure myself;
That I am worth something.

But I am afraid to tell you this,
I don't dare. I am afraid to.
I am afraid that your glance will not be
Followed by love and acceptance.
I'm afraid you'll think less of me,
That you'll laugh at me and your laugh would kill me.
I'm afraid that deep down I'm nothing,
That I'm no good,
And that you will see this and reject me.
So I play my game, my desperate game,
And a trembling child within.
And so begins the parade of masks,
And my life becomes a front.

I dislike hiding. Honestly.
I dislike the superficial game I am playing,
The phony game. I'd really like to be genuine,
Spontaneous, and me.
But you've got to help me.
You've got to hold out your hand,
Even when that's the last thing I seem to want.
Only you can wipe away from my eyes,
The blank stare of breathing death.
Only you can call me into aliveness;
Each time you're kind and gentle, and encouraging.
Each time you try to understand because you care.
My heart grows wings, very small wings
Very feeble wings but wings.
With your sensitivity and sympathy,

And your power of understanding,
You breathe life into me.
I want you to know that.

I want you to know how important you are to me,
How you can be the creator of the person that is me,
If you choose. Please choose to.
You alone can break down the wall,
Behind which I tremble.
You alone can remove my mask.
You alone can release me from my shadow-world
   of panic and uncertainty,
From my lonely person. Do not pass me by.
Please do not pass me by.
It will not be easy for you.
A long conviction of worthlessness builds strong walls.
The nearer you approach me, the blinder I strike back.
I fight against the very thing I cry out for . . .
But I am told that love is stronger than walls,
And in this lies my hope.
Please try to beat down those walls with firm hands,
But with gentle hands, for a child is very sensitive.
Who am I, you may wonder.
I am someone you know very well. . . .
For I am everyone you meet.

What Teens
Need Most
from Their
Parents

One

Teens Need Their Parents to ...

Love Each Other

T eens tell me this in many different ways and forms, but they tell it to me all the time: "I feel more secure when mom and dad love each other. When I know they are in love, it raises my self-esteem. I don't worry so much about what the future will bring—the possibility of nuclear war or that I won't find a job when I get out of school or that I won't get into a good college—when I know mom and dad are secure."

Psychologists agree that a husband and wife's relationship will have a strong impact on their children: The young people who know mom and dad love each other deeply will have better images of themselves.

How can your teens know if you love your mate? Show them! Hold hands with your spouse, kiss (with discretion) in front of them, and hug. Someone once said it takes four or five hugs a day just to exist, seven or eight for maintenance, and ten for growth. Make certain you both grow!

Did you know that there is a difference between loving your mate and being "in love" with your mate? Don't leave your spouse (or your children) guessing when it comes to affection. Show it daily. Keep the fire in your romance, and both your children and your marriage will benefit.

Your spouse, next to God and yourself, is the most important person to you. Did you know it's okay to let your children know that? Dad, let your son and daughter know that mom comes first. Mom, you *can* tell your teens, "I'll spend time with you in a minute, after I do this for [or with] dad." After all, the two of you will have to live with each other for many more years than you will have the kids. Don't sacrifice your marriage to the demands of a child. After all, most teens won't stay home much past thirty-three or thirty-four years!

How sad to see parents who barely tolerate each other, yet stay together, caught in the same habit and life-style for years and years. Twenty years later, the marriage falls apart because they haven't done old things in a new way and life has become boring and stagnant. Keep some life in your marriage.

Love your mate. Fall back in love with your husband or wife. Begin by doing the small things, like opening doors for your wife or making a special effort to look good for your husband. Those little things bring about big results and big differences—they also take care of the big problems.

A Word to Single Parents

But what if you are a single parent? Does this leave you in a real bind, dooming your children to a sense of low self-esteem? Not at all. To raise your children with a good self-image, follow these three steps:

1. Have a strong spiritual relationship with God. If your children do not see that you believe in something greater than your problems, they will not know that there is something greater for them to hang onto in their own troubles.

2. Have a high self-esteem (and never put down the other parent in a divorce situation). Your children want you to believe in your ability to handle life as it comes. Make the best of it, look up, count your blessings, and feel good about yourself. Too many people look at the dark side of life, when they don't need to. Be an example to your teens, and it will help them feel good about themselves.

3. Give your teens both time and love.

When I asked my uncle George what helped him raise two healthy, drug-free teens, he stopped and thought, then replied, "It would have to be *the time we spent together*. In the summer we would rent a little, fifteen-dollar-a-weekend cottage on Lake Michigan. It wasn't anything fancy, but we were all there. Or if I had a business trip, I would try to arrange to have them come with me.

"One of the houses we lived in was far away from any others, and we always spent time together, enjoying one another's company. When our son asked my advice on something, I would first ask what the parents of his friends advised them. He would often reply that their parents were too busy to talk and share with them."

Amazingly, the reason for some of the greatest successes in families, as well as in life, may lie in the little things. Spending time together, enjoying each other doesn't look so little when you realize that it *takes time*. Today's one- and two-parent families don't have much, if any, spare time, but this precious commodity means the most to young people as they grow up.

Two

Teens Need Their Parents to . . .

Know that Love Must Be Nurtured

Young people seem to know so much more than we give them credit for. Instinctively they understand that love's just like a springtime flower: Both are living things—they have a chance to grow or to die.

This year we missed the beautiful fragrance of our lilac bush. During a warm spell, it started putting out buds, all set for spring. But a severe frost followed that balmy spell, and the buds just couldn't make it. For many people, love works just like that. Someone seems to love them, and they begin to open up, only to find that person doesn't really have the time or caring to let them flower. It's just as if they'd been hit by a frost.

Give your "plants"—the people you love—the right conditions to grow. We need to talk and sing to those we love, to nourish them. Humor fertilizes love; so does a sparkle in the eye, an "I love you," or a "you're the greatest."

Remember the Little Things

When my wife and I were dating, there was hardly a door she could handle. I opened every single one. "Here, honey." "Here we go." "Yeah, right this way." Naturally she could barely handle them herself: Holly's only a frail five foot ten inches!

Spouses appreciate the little things. Open those doors, men, and show the same common courtesy you showed before you said, "I do." Stand up when your wife sits down, just before a meal; pull back her chair for her. Help her do the dishes after dinner. Make a game out of everyday chores around the house. Treat your wife at least as well as you'd treat your golfing buddy.

Isn't it amazing how we are rarely late for a game of golf or something else we enjoy doing with the guys, but when it comes to going out with our wives, being ten or twenty minutes late is nothing? Many times husbands have the attitude: *She's my wife, and we live together, so it doesn't matter. We've been living like this for fifteen years, and she hasn't complained yet.* (Maybe she has, and he just hasn't paid attention!)

Motivational speaker Denis Waitley describes that attitude of caring for a wife this way, "She's just like my car. I change the oil only when I have to. When the dipstick is low, I take her in. If she starts leaking oil or throws a rod, I call the mechanic and ask what's wrong with this thing." Marriage doesn't have to work that way. How much better to get the checkups ahead of time. You'd do that if you owned a $40,000 racing car—a finely tuned machine that deserves to run smoothly all the time. If it didn't run well, you'd tune it up, investing some more money in it, because it's a vital part of your life. How much *more* important to have that attitude toward your spouse, because he or she is an integral part of your life, happiness, and inner peace!

Don't Be Afraid of Change

If I forget to water my roses, they won't grow. If I fail to fertilize them, they won't get nearly as large. If I don't use pesticide on them, to keep the bugs away, they'll look like lace by the time I want to pick them (and the littlest bugs do the worst damage).

Love's like that. It needs care and attention—and *change*. (Leave your flowers alone and see what you get.) Your son or daughter wants you to know that things can change around the house: new activities, different games, other TV shows. Variety quickens love. Put your furniture in different places. My wife always does. (In fact I think she has to do it twice a week, just to breathe normally.) How exciting to come home late, after one of my speaking engagements. I come in, have a quick snack, go upstairs, make my way to the bed—and four new chairs and a solid new end table jump into my path. Life should be like that . . . stubbed toes and all.

One lady described change this way: "I love it. You should have seen this morning. I was so mad at him at the time, but it's beautiful now that I look back on it. There I was in the shower, and he dropped a jar of ice-cold water on my head, over the top of the shower curtain." She chuckled. "Life isn't boring at least!" Keeping the life in our marriages means what I call "adding spice to make it nice."

I'll never forget one evening, at a public seminar I'd helped sponsor and I spoke at. To the 2,000 people who came, I talked about stepping out of your comfort zone, trying new things and daring to be different, because change is healthy and exciting. Halfway through the program, two ladies walked up to me, smiling from ear to ear.

"We've only been here just a couple of hours, and we've already got our money's worth," one declared.

I asked what she meant, and she responded, "You know how you shared that it is all right to try new things, and it won't kill you? We went down the hallway to the ladies' rest room, and there was a long line. Obviously it would have taken us at least forty minutes to get in there, so we went on up to the second floor. There was no one in the men's room, and it was great!"

When I told them to try new things, I really didn't have *that* kind of change in mind, but I'll bet those two didn't have a boring breakfast the next day. They probably had a chuckle when the coffeepot didn't work. "Who cares?" they may have asked. At noon, if someone honked at them or pulled out in front of their car or if the light didn't change quickly enough when they drove home from work or if the weather was too hot or cold, it probably didn't bother them as much.

Change, try new things, be different. Teens like to be with others their age, because younger folks don't mind laughing. They enjoy having fun and just plain goofing off sometimes. As we get older we become so rigid and stale, sturdy and clockwise. Maybe one of the reasons I get along with teens so well is that I have a great management style and organizational ability. Quite often I run my life this way: ready . . . shoot . . . aim! I have to speak to see what's on my mind.

Does the idea of breaking habit patterns and creating new ones seem threatening? Look at it this way: Do any of us wear the same shoes we wore in second grade or the same shirt we wore when we were twelve years old? Of course not! That would be crazy. Well, how about the way we raise our children and keep our families together? Have we changed some of our old, worn-out, hard-to-fit, cramping habits and life-styles? Or have we stayed back in second grade?

Some of us are like the man who started a new job, wearing

brand-new clothes. During the first day on the job, while handling some problems, his head started spinning and his eyes felt as if they were going to pop out of his head. He put down the phone, rested a few minutes, then tried again. The same thing happened. When it continued on the next day, the man went to the company doctor, who suggested it might be caused by stress and had the man try another job. He did, but the same thing happened a few minutes later.

The company doctor didn't know what to do, so he sent the man to a specialist. Now specialists are meant to find something wrong, and this one did: He found a rare disease. The doctor called it rare because he didn't often have the symptoms of a spinning head and popping eyes put together. He gave the disease a name and the man six months to live.

Upset and confused, the man went to talk to a friend, who suggested that he really start living. Starting that day, the man made some changes in his life. He canceled his life-insurance policy and got the money (he wanted his death to be a real tragedy) and started traveling with his new automobile. He bought a place on the ocean front, and he went one day to get the tailor-made clothes he had always wanted. While fitting the shirt, the tailor said, "What shirt sleeve and neck size do you wear?"

"I wear a fifteen–thirty-five," the man answered.

"Oh, no," the tailor responded. "I just measured you, and you are definitely a sixteen–thirty-six."

"No, I've always been a fifteen–thirty-five," the man explained.

The tailor cried, "If you wear a shirt sleeve of thirty-five and a neck size of fifteen, your head is going to be spinning and your eyes will feel as if they could pop right out of your head."

That man didn't change his shirt size and only had six months more to live. What will happen if we don't change some of our habits?

Remember what Reggie Smith says: *If you always do what you've always done, you'll always get what you've always gotten.*

Three

Keep Talking to Them

One of the messages teens give me to pass on to their parents is, "Let's keep talking." Quite often this is the number-one problem they share. They come up to me and say things like, "I wish mom and dad would talk with me. I wish I could go to them. I wish my parents would listen. We don't talk anymore. I never talk to my parents." I've heard so many variations on this theme that I *expect* to hear it. The boy or girl who comes up to tell me how well he can talk to his dad or she can talk to mom is the exception that proves the rule. A rare teen can talk to mom or dad and find that parent treating him or her as a growing human being, not just a short adult.

Sometimes communication in the family seems like the situation of one family that went to a restaurant. The waitress came over and took the parents' order, then said, "What shall I get the little boy?" The father answered, "The boy will have a hot dog."

"I want a hamburger, daddy, I want a hamburger," the boy cried. "Give the boy a hot dog," overruled the man. The waitress asked the boy, "Son, what would you like to drink?" Turning to his daddy, the youngster exclaimed, "Daddy, she thinks I'm a real person!"

Tips to Better Communication

Studies have shown that poor communication causes most family and business failures. To improve the situation in your family, try making use of these ideas:

TELL ME EXACTLY WHAT YOU MEAN.   One common road-block to effective communication forces us onto a bumpy path when we don't say what we mean. Because we see things differently from the way our teens do, as we talk we have to make certain that both of us have the same perception of the situation.

Suppose a teen comes to dad and says, "I'm going out now." Dad, wrapped up in the movie he's watching (or book he's reading or the expression of gratefulness he's attempting to give), says, "All right. Make sure you come home on time."

With a response like that, it's possible his son will come in at some time other than the one he had in mind. To him, ten o'clock may seem the proper teen curfew, but his son may think twelve would be just fine. A better response to the son's announcement would have been, "I'll expect you home by ten, okay?" Then dad had better listen carefully to make sure which side of midnight his son thinks that *ten* is!

If a mother tells her daughter, "You really let me down the other day," the girl won't know what she said or did that caused her mom to say those words. Instead mom needs to tell her teen *exactly* what she did wrong and what she can do differently next time.

When a dad says to his daughter, "Let's get together and talk about your grades this week," he leaves her up in the air. She still won't know what he has in mind and may not do anything about it. Only when dad says, "I'm ready, how about you?" can she know what's up. Remember, teens are rapidly changing human beings, but they are not adults. Until that father shows his daughter how to negotiate a time to talk, she probably won't learn how to do it.

Teens tell me that deep down, they know their parents love them, but the adults don't *tell* them. Saying what you mean means *saying it*. Don't hold it all inside. If you feel hurt or happy, your teen has a right to know. For example, how will your son be able to tell his future wife that he loves her if he has never heard you say that to your wife?

Use these three keys to say it.

1. Talking with teens is like setting goals: You must be *specific*. Say what you mean; then make certain they've understood. Don't drop it with a simple question. Ask them to *explain* what you mean.

2. Next, keep your goals *flexible*. Sometimes we all change our minds. If you have to alter direction in the midst of demanding something from your teen, communicate that.

3. As you would in other goals, engage in small successes. Communicate each idea in a short, precise sentence, rather than covering three or four concepts in one long sentence.

    For example, suppose your daughter plans a trip. It's better to (1) remind her to check the oil in the car (and make certain she knows how to do it); (2) go over the map ahead of time, to make sure she knows what turns to make; (3) ask her to check the rattle in the left rear tire, at the service station, before she leaves on the trip.

If you cover all three items separately and ask what your directions mean, your daughter will have a clearer idea of her responsibilities than if you say, "Have fun on the trip, don't forget that left-rear-tire rattle, look over the map, and if you don't check the oil, the engine may freeze up." If you say all this as she gets ready to rush out the door, she may feel so nervous about the engine freezing up that she forgets the tire and map. Or she may feel you have no time to go over the specifics, decide she's incapable, or experience a lot of stress. She might even allow the car to get in trouble just to hear you say "I told you so."

Say what you *really* mean!

REMEMBER: TONE MEANS MORE THAN WORDS. When you share with *anyone*, though your verbal message might be important, the tone tells even more. In fact experts say 38 percent of communication comes from your tone of voice. If you say, "All right, I love you," or, "Okay, let's talk," or, "Sure I want to listen, tell me about it," but your tone says something else, you're in trouble. Kids are especially sensitive to the tone of your voice.

BODY LANGUAGE IS WORTH A THOUSAND WORDS. If your words conflict with your body language, guess which one your teens will hear? You can't really say, "I love you," with your arms folded. If you're looking away from your son as you say, "Yeah, we're going to make it. Dad will stay with you, no matter what," don't wonder why he doesn't seem too enthusiastic about your encouragement. Nonverbal actions speak louder than your words; they make up 55 percent of your communication.

DON'T CRITICIZE AND COMPLIMENT IN THE SAME SENTENCE. When you build someone up, don't tear him down in the same sentence. If you tell your teen, "I'm proud of you, you did a great job on the lawn, but you left your room a mess," all he will hear is the part of the sentence after *but*. Separate the criticisms from the compliments. Let each stand alone. Start a new sentence before you object to anything.

SHOW UNCONDITIONAL LOVE IN YOUR COMMENTS. Don't make your love seem to be based on your teens' actions. If you say something positive only when they do well and say nothing at all when they don't, your teens will assume you love them only when you praise them. If they've gone the extra mile for someone, try to say something like, "That must make you feel good inside," instead of "You make me proud when . . . ," because that praise is unconditional. Use expressions that give your teens inner motivation, not just the external kind which works when they make the team or get the good report card or get voted the most popular person in the class. Don't let them fall into the trap of only having motivation when someone builds them up or pats them on the back.

If you say something like, "That must make you feel good inside," you give your teens something to fall back on the next time they do something and no one around recognizes it. Such inner courage and determination are two of the best weapons a person can go through life with. They provide the ammunition that says, "I've got within me the power to make it in life. Through my problems, and on the days when I don't get a standing ovation, I can take it, because I feel good inside."

MAKE SOME CHANGES IN YOUR LIFE. When I talk to teens, I tell them to keep talking to their parents. "Meet them halfway," I encourage them. "This is a time in life when you're developing physically, mentally, emotionally, and in other ways, too. You're changing now more than you ever will for the rest of your life. It's a rapid, scary thing, and you need to communicate with your parents."

"You're right," most teens answer. "We *are* the ones who are changing. *Our parents haven't changed in years.*" Young people understand the need to change, grow, be spontaneous, do something new. Do you?

Try it in your own life. Take a new route to work. When someone's not smiling, don't let that affect you. Just say, "Good morning, smiley." (It gets people almost every time.) If someone asks how you're doing, don't say, "Fine." Look him in the eye and say, "Better and better." If he asks if you've been sick, tell him you don't have to be sick to get better. When I said that to one woman, she said, "I don't know how bad things have been, but you're looking all right now."

Change the way you get up in the morning. One football player told me that the first thing he does every morning is roll out of bed, onto his knees, and say a good-morning prayer to thank the Lord for the day, his abilities, God's love for him, what God did for him and will do for him. He said it changes his whole outlook. When he forgets to do that, practices go badly and relationships don't do well. Those few minutes set the foundation for his whole day.

Why not try using a new way to tell your kids you love them and want to talk? Let them know you're in this thing together.

If it's been a while since you've spoken to your son, tell him you know it's been a long time, but you want to become his biggest fan and teammate. Explain to your daughter that you care about her and who she is. Let your teen know it will take a while to rebuild and strengthen the relationship, but you are ready and waiting, with two listening ears. Share that you find it hard to talk and that you don't understand a lot of things in your son or daughter's life. Speak honestly, as you would to a friend, working partner, or teammate. Explain some of the things that really bug you about your teen. Tell your young person that you are not perfect, but you want some help in talking things out.

Do you know what all this will mean to your child? *Teens desperately want their parents to share about their imperfections.* They understand that mom and dad don't know everything. Show them that you are big enough to ask them to be with you along the way.

Teach Your Teens That It's Okay to Discuss and Disagree. Once you've started to talk, be open with your son or daughter. Teens need to know that it is absolutely okay to discuss thoughts, situations, and problems as well as to disagree with your thoughts and solutions when they need to get something off their chests. Just as an employer should leave communication open with his staff, your son or daughter also wants the freedom to set an appointment for time when you can be alone and discuss what he or she feels mad about (or resents or appreciates or feels about you or doesn't understand).

I once went to a meeting where I spoke to a number of very successful businessmen. These executives were truly at the top of their fields, earning an awful lot of money. On top of all that, they had giant egos.

I'll never forget how the meeting began. My speech was well prepared. I had talked with several people ahead of time, so I knew I would be giving them interesting information and some helpful tips they needed to do an even better job. I opened with some great stories and some good material, trying to get audience involvement. But something went wrong.

Ten minutes into my program, I realized these people must

have felt that because I was only thirty-two years old, I could not offer them helpful suggestions. I had not earned the right.

For three or four minutes I tried some audience-participation ploys that almost always work; these, too, went over like a lead balloon. I didn't know quite what to do.

Finally, about fourteen minutes into my one-hour presentation, I became very quiet, looked at them, and said, "We've got a problem. I came in here today with a very healthy self-esteem. I felt very good about myself. I love what I do. Because I work as hard as I do at it, I feel that I'm good at what I do. For over fifteen years I have been running my own business and have shared the platform with many of the top speakers and authors in the country. In the last fourteen minutes, I've found it nearly impossible to communicate with you. I would just like to ask all of you one question before we go any further."

At this point, you could have heard a pin drop. It was the last thing they expected me to do—level with them and come right forward and say, "What is going on? Preparing for this talk and meeting, with the coordinator who hired me, all I heard was how sophisticated you are, how important you are, how much money you are making, and how I better have usable meat, not just fluff, for you today, or I would never speak to you again. My question is, 'If it is this hard for *me*, a very high achiever with a healthy self-esteem, how hard is it for your employees to talk with you?' "

I added, "I came in here with my self-esteem about a ten, on a one to ten scale. It is now about a four, and I don't want it to go any lower!"

They were awestruck by the truth. I said, "I would like all of you to stand up and come sit down in the front." (They had been scattered throughout the entire room, arms folded and taking no notes.)

At that point, I shared what my responsibilities were to them for the next forty-five minutes. I was to present usable ideas that they could put into practice in the next twenty-four hours; to do it in an inspirational, interesting, and enjoyable way, so that they would be able to say at the end of the program, "The time went fast; the ideas were good; I feel better about me now that I've been here."

Then I mentioned, "I also think that each one of you has a responsibility, as an audience, for the next forty-five minutes. You should listen attentively, ask questions, take notes, and be the best listener you possibly can be, as well as give me honest feedback as to the good and the bad of this meeting, when it is finished."

From that time, the meeting went smoothly. I got high ratings. The response was beautiful, and several business people asked me to come to talk to their companies as a result of our time together.

Do you see what happened? I simply wanted to be able to *discuss and disagree at any time*. The men in that meeting didn't know that that was my right. I had to just take it.

At home your teens have the same problem I had in the meeting, when you are reading the paper or involved with your favorite sporting activity or thinking about work or engrossed with all the responsibilities of being a parent. Your son or daughter can't get through.

Let your teens feel free to discuss their feelings and their problems, their joys and frustrations. Most often they don't know they can disagree and actually say, "Why are you not listening? Why do you do it this way? I think it should be done another way." If we just put our families on the same basis as we do our business or profession, we would have a wider channel of communication in which to meet our children halfway. Teenagers need practice disagreeing with people in a tactful way. We have given them firsthand experience of disagreeing tactfully if we discuss without shouting or getting angry and keep our emotions down. When the time comes for them to disagree with their mates or about something they do not believe in on the job, they will draw upon this experience.

Conversation Starters

What if it's been a long time since you've discussed something with your son or daughter? Sometimes parents have a hard time sharing with their teens; perhaps they have some trouble getting a perspective on their relationship with them, or they just don't know where to start. I'd like to suggest that you use the following family test to discover more about you and your teen. First you'll evaluate your own strong and weak areas, while your teen looks at his or hers. Then you'll share what you've found out about yourselves. Be honest in looking at yourselves, because without honesty, you cannot realistically communicate your inner self. No one is perfect, so don't try to pretend you are. Everyone has some good points, though—try to uncover some new ones.

In addition, do not become harshly critical in your evaluations of each other. This test should be a time of fun and discovery, not one family's civil war. Come to see the personalities you each have and to appreciate them more.

The second section of the family test focuses on the relationships you have with one another and the things you would change in your family. Once again, use this to build your family and the understanding you have of each other. Make it an honest, open time of sharing.

Family Test

Parent's Name _____

Strong Points
Describe your skills and abilities, such as writing talent, good organizer, punctual, likes math, plays baseball well, sense of humor, getting along with people, and so on.

1.
2.
3.
4.
5.
6.
7.
8.
9.
10.

Weak Points
Include areas for improvement—any skills or areas in which you could do better

1.
2.
3.
4.
5.

Child's Name _____

Strong Points

1.
2.
3.
4.
5.
6.
7.
8.
9.
10.

Weak Points

1.
2.
3.
4.
5.

SOMETHING TO TALK ABOUT.   After you've looked at your strong and weak areas, talk about other things that may be on your minds. Here are some topics you may wish to use.

1. I wish you understood . . . about me.
2. If I had a magic wand, I would change . . . in our family.
3. If I had a magic wand, I would change . . . in the world.
4. I always appreciate it when you. . . .
5. To me, a hypocrite is someone who. . . .
6. A hero is someone who. . . .

 7. Some of my heroes are. . . .
 8. I love you because. . . .
 9. I love God because. . . .
10. I am excited about the future because. . . .
11. I am afraid of the future because. . . .
12. Activities I like doing with you are. . . .
13. I am most proud of. . . .
14. Traditions in our family I love the most are. . . .
15. I admire you most because. . . .
16. I need you most when. . . .
17. I need to be alone most when. . . .
18. When I say "everything is okay" I really mean. . . .
19. What I think about . . . (*pornography/sex before marriage/love/child abuse/alcohol/drugs/ and so on*).
20. A goal that is very important to me is. . . .

Make Use of What You've Learned

Now that you know a little more about communication in the family, begin to put it into practice. Take time to use these tips that can make a good family life better and can literally transform a bad one. Find out what your teens think, what bothers them, and what makes them happy. In addition, open yourselves to them, because communication is a two-way street.

Once you begin to know each other better and share your lives more fully, you'll never want to go back to your old ways!

Four

Give Them Unconditional Acceptance and Love

In the last chapter I encouraged you to show unconditional love in your comments to your son or daughter, but such love has to go much farther in order to make your teen really feel secure. Each young person needs to know that he or she will consistently get total, accepting love from mom and dad. No matter what his performance, your son needs to know you will always say, "It doesn't matter, you're still our child." Your daughter needs to know she'll always remain a part of the family, no matter what.

Maybe you've had to turn to "tough love," but you still need to accept your teen and love him, despite the circumstances, if you plan on getting him back or keeping him. Although her performance may not excite you, and his friends may be wild, you have to accept and love your teens. In those difficult situations, love the doer, not the deed.

When my four-year-old daughter does something wrong, I've

47

got to let her know that I love her, but what she did cannot be accepted. I tell her, "You are getting spanked because . . . , but daddy loves you." Even at that age, the achiever and the achievement are two different things. Why shouldn't the principle stay the same for your teens?

Forgive your teens for the little things (or even the big ones) that they do. By separating us from our sins, if we just accept what He did for us on the cross, almost 2,000 years ago, the Creator of the universe has taught us how to forgive. Yet we find it difficult to reach out in the same way to a teenage son or daughter who has not acted like a thirty-year-old. Our teens have forgiven and forgotten many of our errors. How can we do less for them?

The young people I talk to share that they don't want mom and dad to love them more if they get an A on a paper or make the team or seem popular in school. But many of them need and work for parental approval, but see it only in their dreams. Keep telling and showing your teens that you will always be there for them. You wouldn't believe the stories children tell of parents who have said, "If you do that again [or go out with that person again or leave this house and do that one more time], don't ever come back." I think that may be one of the biggest mistakes a parent can make. Perhaps in a situation such as drugs, rehabilitation for a violent or law-breaking act, or in a case of certain moral standards, that might become necessary, but in most cases a parent should not make leaving an option. Teens need a home to turn to, and need parents as allies. Your home is your child's refuge.

I know some youngsters who, at ten to thirteen years of age have been told, "Do this—or leave." Those few words gave them the message: *As long as you do exactly what we want you to do, you can live here; but don't give us any trouble, or you're out.*

From the way it sounds, any group of people who live that way hate each other. A family that wants to stick together has to work as a team. Be like a skein of geese; they fly 75 percent farther because they do it together, in a V formation.

Never give your kids the alternative of not coming back home. I know some who have told me they didn't go back, they can't go back, and they won't go back. America has an outrageous runaway scene. According to radio personality Paul Harvey, in 1982 over 5,000 cults and occult groups in this nation had over 3 million members. Most of those were young people who no longer lived at home. In the same year, he said, there were over 1 million runaways—of an average age of fourteen years old.

Many of those kids create the serious crime in America. According to a 1980 FBI Uniform Crime Report, 27 percent of those arrested for murder were age fifteen or under. Forty-two percent of those arrested for rape had not yet reached their sixteenth birthday. Children of this age have accounted for 44 percent of the robbery arrests and aggravated assault arrests; for 54 percent of the burglary arrests; for 72 percent of the arson arrests. Kids like that are crying out for help.

Every teen needs total, unconditional acceptance and love—including yours. No matter what happens to your teen, make that love available. When your son does something that drives you wild, start by realizing that the person is different from the action. Just as God does, you can hate the sin and love the sinner. When your daughter does something you'd told her not to, remember that she still needs all your love.

Teens aren't alone in needing acceptance. Mom and dad, you need your friends', spouse's, and colleagues' (and even your teens') love and assurance. You've done some things wrong in life, and other people have given you a second chance . . . and a third and fourth. If you do something wrong at the office, you wouldn't want your boss to stay mad for two months. Keep that in mind when you deal with your young folks.

Teens need that same kind of acceptance—desperately. For these few years, they face a tough time in life, and when they say things like, "Stay away. . . . I don't need you. . . . I can do it on my own," they need you most.

Five

Teens Need Their Parents to . . .

Be an Example

Y oung people today seem to have a sixth sense when it comes to knowing if someone's for real. Without any trouble they can pick up on the person who isn't sincere—because they look at his actions. When we say something but don't act in a way that supports it, they know we're hypocrites—no one else has to tell them.

As parents you can actively teach your children or not teach them. But by the time your son or daughter has reached those teen years, he or she has begun to understand things, even if you haven't said a word. Still, one young man who had gotten beyond his teens explained his remaining confusion this way: "As I grew out of my teens, for a while I was actually mad that my parents did not teach me the Lord's Prayer, 'The Star-Spangled Banner,' or anything about how America was founded and on what principles we stand. I never knew why communism was bad, and I never knew anything about politics or how to make up my own choice on capital punishment. I often wondered why I kept hearing from my parents that there is no such thing as a free handout in America, that we have to earn everything we get; then I watched people keep playing the state lottery games. Why does the older generation continually blame us kids for being no good when very few teenagers run the bars or X-rated movie shows or deal in drugs or gang warfare on a large scale?"

His parents certainly never taught him some important things, but he'd also seen right through some ideas they'd probably tried to impress on him. He'd looked at examples around him.

In our society today, kids know the meaning of *hypocrisy*, and they see it acted out every day. The last thing they need is to have their own parents showing them more of it. Instead, they need examples of the positive ways to act. How will they know, if you don't show them?

Walk Your Talk

As far as today's teens are concerned, if you don't walk it, don't talk it; if you don't practice it, don't preach it. They can easily see through words when actions don't agree. For example, teens know that alcohol and marijuana are both drugs, so if you drink to excess and then try to condemn your son for using marijuana, he won't hear those words. "If you can get drunk," your daughter might ask, "why can't I get high? What's the difference?" With all we know about the negative effects of alcohol, how could you answer her questions honestly?

While we're on the subject of alcohol, you may not know that it's the number-one killer of our young people. Some parents say things like, "I'd rather have them home drinking than out doing those drugs," but in light of the results of scientific studies and the influence alcohol has had on society, those words are pure ignorance. Our young people need to know about the troubles of families invaded by alcohol. We need to tell them about the lost jobs and lost lives, the broken hearts and homes, and the tears and endless hours during which a parent (or a child) wonders what has become of a person who's loved.

LIMIT TV. On the home front, we need to show our young people that too much TV hurts all of us—both parents and children. We can't have close home lives if we spend too much time watching what other artificial families do, but never spend any time with our own.

In order to limit and control the use of the TV in your home, start becoming an example. Make up some coupons (maybe ten a person, per week) that each represent an hour of television time. Every time you watch for an hour, you give up a coupon, till they are gone. No more coupons, no more TV for that week. Dad, show your son or daughter you *really* mean business by using up all your coupons the first week of September and missing "Monday Night Football." When you do that, your kids will say, "He's in this thing for real. . . . I'll play the game, too." Then make certain you spend that extra time together!

WALK THE LIFE OF FAITH. When it comes to faith, don't send your kids to church—*take them*. Be that example. If you want to have your kids run to God and look for His guidance, show them that you do. It could have the same kind of impact one father had on the life of his child:

> My father took very seriously the role of being spiritual leader in our family. Every morning, long before we got up for school, he would have his own quiet time for prayer and Bible study. He also wanted us to read the Bible every day

and spend time quietly reflecting over our day's activities, asking and thanking God for our requests and needs. However, he never pushed it on us. He just quietly did his thing.

By the time I was in my teen years, I noticed how, in everyday conversation, my father would mention how God had allowed this or that or how we had been blessed. He might say that we should be more like Abraham or tell how Joseph would have handled a particular situation. It was just a natural thing for us to be drawn to the very activity he wanted to lead us to in the first place. He didn't actually push us, but flavored his desire in such a way that we were hungry for it.

I now have my quiet time every day, and I can see why my father was such a peaceful man. I can see the importance of living out our lives instead of just talking about it.

When I asked my father, he mentioned that, yes, he wanted us to read the Bible and spend time getting to know God. But he wasn't going to waste his thoughts worrying about us. He was going to get closer to God himself instead.

The end result was beautiful. We've all learned that God is here to help us. With our small, daily time (maybe only five minutes), we can grow just as our father did.

What a contrast such a testimony makes to the parents who show up at a Wednesday-night family service, but don't bother to stay for them. Mom or dad pulls up and lets the kids out to play the games and learn the Scriptures. An hour later, the same parent has to stand around for ten or fifteen minutes, waiting for the end of the service. Considering the inconvenience, it probably would have been easier to stay, after all. If mom and dad *had* stayed, the youngsters also would never get the idea that God didn't mean all that much to their parents. Young people need a positive example in faith.

SHOW THEM WHAT IT MEANS TO BE HONEST.   Honesty can show in little things like answering the phone. Don't tell your teens that honesty is the way—the only way—and that you built your business by it, then tell them (when the phone rings and it's not convenient for you to answer) to say, "He's not here." Be honest. Don't compromise in the little things, because they make way for the big things in life.

THEY WILL LEARN FROM YOUR ACTIONS.   If you encourage your son or daughter, he or she will grow up to encourage others. If you criticize your teens, they will become critical of others. If you get mad at others, behind their backs, you can expect your teens to do the same. In short, whatever you do, they will do, too.

A little boy sat in the backseat of the car as his mom drove him to church one Sunday morning. His daddy usually drove the car, and as they crossed the bridge, the boy missed something. "Mama," he asked. "Where are all the @#$%& today?"

She answered, "Oh, honey, they're not out when your daddy's not here!"

Kids watch every action, see every move. They hear the little words, sentences, and put-downs. In addition they hear the praises and watch the positive examples.

A young man shared the influence his parents had on his bad habit of bragging. Although they didn't confront him directly, they encouraged him to make a change by their example.

"It seems that I was always the very best at sports and at academics," he told me. "In our youth group at church, for example, I was always one of the fastest to run a certain race, and I always had an easy time of memorizing the assigned verses. Without realizing, I would walk with my head tall and say little things like, 'Yes, I'm always one of the first to get done,' or, 'I get more points than anyone for remembering verses.'

"My parents could see this and handled it so beautifully that I didn't even realize it at the time.

"At night my dad would give an example of something he was good at on the job. He shared how it was important for him not to gloat, put anyone down, or hurt others' feelings because of it. My mother also would share how fortunate we were for our house, certain talents, or certain blessings and she told us how we should be thankful for these.

"This was at the very time when I was getting fairly big-headed. I was about fourteen years old. It took several months, but I remember almost like a flash waking up and saying to my mom and dad, 'I've been bragging a lot, haven't I? I don't think that's the way God wants me to be.'

"As I look back now, they knew it all along. But the way they presented it to me made it easy to digest and live with. I am still thankful to them to this very day."

HELP YOUR TEENS CHOOSE.   "None of your children were born winners or losers, but they were *all* born choosers," says Reggie Smith. We all get to make decisions in life, and especially in America, we have many options. Give your teens a good role model to help in making those choices.

Six

Listen to Them

Almost every day I'm out in communities and schools, I hear, "Tell my mom and dad that when I'm in trouble or hurting, when I need help, I need them to *listen*." I'd like to give you a few steps you can use when your child hurts:

1. Don't give advice.
2. Just listen, hold that child, hurt with him or her, be there, but don't say anything.
3. Keep telling your teen you love him or her and that it will turn out okay.

My dad used one sentence with me many times. He shared it with me when I came home and told him my dog had just died, when I couldn't make the team, when I cried because other kids made fun of me. When I lost $25,000 in one day, from a bad business venture; when I had to admit that my wife and I had to walk away from our first home, losing almost $10,000, because I hadn't been aware of the wording of the mortgage; when I told him the doctors said Holly and I would never have any children (our daughter is adopted)—even then he used those same words. They are: *If this is the worst thing that ever happens to you, I think we'll make it.* He always said *we'll,* because he meant he would always be there with me. *No matter what the loss, the hurt, or the heartache, it's over,* his words implied. *If that's the worst thing that happens, we will make it.* He focused on the future, looking toward tomorrow. We could make it.

Guess what? We did.

Focus on Your Teen

A wise person once said that our Creator gave us two ears and only one mouth, and when we communicate with our children we should use them in that proportion. Listening is one of the greatest communication skills, yet seldom do we see a course of study or a class that will teach us how to do it better; we haven't gotten much training on it.

If you're like the average person, when someone talks to you, you probably feel so concerned about all the important points you want to share, all the ideas milling around in your mind—what *your* vacation was like or how *you* learned so much from so-and-so—that you forget it's time to listen. As we deal with our children, we can't afford to give in to all those distractions—we need to pay attention.

When we truly listen, our eyes focus on the speaker, instead of moving around the room. If we show a clear interest, along with concern, love, and caring, our teens will begin to share. By encouraging them, we can get them to open up and tell us why they hurt, why they feel life's no longer worth living, about a drinking or drug problem, about how much effort it takes to stand up against having sex with a boyfriend or girl friend.

Then they may want to know if we've ever faced the same problem. What an opportunity for any parent—an invitation to communicate!

Head Versus Heart

A friend of mine shared this exciting concept about parent-child communication. Perhaps it can help you understand the differences between you and your child, when you try to explain something.

Suppose your son comes to you with a request—whether it involves using the car, wanting to spend time with certain friends, or permission to have a physical item. While he speaks, he will do everything possible to make you listen to his feelings. As you hear the case he pleads, you may feel a gut reaction to it. Now look at what goes on.

Your son tries to convince you on the basis of how he *feels*. You respond with an argument that attempts to convince him of the *facts*. As he pleads from the heart, you plead from the head. Now comes the key to communication in such a situation: *To the extent to which you hear and truly listen to your child's feelings on a subject, he will listen to and hear your facts on it.* Remember, if you hear his feelings, he'll hear your facts.

Communication has to be a two-way street. Tune in to your son's feelings about why he needs it, why something hurts him or why he has struggles; only after he sees that you have done that, will he listen to your facts.

Naturally this does not mean that in the end he will agree with you 100 percent and go along with what you would like him to do. However, when you give him your facts, based on this kind of understanding, he will listen more readily, and you may have *some* influence on his thinking.

Also, this kind of attitude makes communication a 100/100 percent situation, not just a 50/50 one. Even if you do not agree, you will understand each other much better.

But what if your teen doesn't seem interested when you try to talk?

WHAT IF THAT DOESN'T WORK?   Daily, whenever I am with teens, they tell me they would give almost anything to tell you what I'm saying here. It's not that they don't care; but you may not hear, because they don't share. They want to, all right, but they don't feel convinced that anyone feels interested. Just like a little child, when you ask, "What's wrong?" they say, "Nothing." But inside their hearts, they wish you'd ask a couple more times. They *want* to share, but they find it very difficult.

If you walk away, saying, "Okay, if that's the way you are going to be—if you don't want to talk, I don't have time to stick around here," they feel hurt. They desperately need mom and dad's love and care, even if they make it hard to give. In a few years your young people will go off to face life alone, and they need the skills parents can give that will enable them to handle the world. Take time to build them with your child.

The kind of communication we're talking about here may not come in a few minutes. To develop it, you may have to use all the patience you can muster. But hang in there—the final results will be worth it.

Seven

Teens Need Their Parents to ...

Be a Secure Door

One of my heroes, Dr. James Dobson, shared this principle on one of his radio programs. Suppose you had a building. During the night it would be locked, but sometime before dawn, a security person would check the doors of the building, to see that they were indeed locked. If you were the security person you'd surely hope they were locked; otherwise it means someone is in there. But until you'd checked, by trying to open the door, you wouldn't know. Dr. Dobson pointed out that our young people are the same way. They always have to test us to see if we'll give in, if we'll budge in our stance. They want to see if we are indeed secure, or if we're just flimsy.

So how do you know when to stand firm and when to give a little? I'd suggest this guideline: *Bend on formalities, but stand firm on principles.* Don't give up only because your teen persists on something.

I'd like to share what this means by giving you a live example. One evening my sister had a date. The boy came to pick her up, and as he pulled out, for about fifteen feet, he slung the gravel in our driveway. It was his first big mistake. (What he didn't know was that right behind them, my father slung gravel for about thirty-three feet.) As the boy drove on he made his second mistake—burning rubber in front of our home, on the way to the movie theater. Even though my dad's car wasn't fast enough to burn rubber, the chase was on. Remember the 1960s TV show "Highway Patrol"? Well, my dad thought he was Broderick Crawford. A few miles from home he pulled that boy's car over. He went to my sister and simply said, "Honey, wouldn't you rather come home with daddy and watch TV with the family, instead of going to the boring movie with your boyfriend?" (I bet you're fairly sure he didn't say it quite that way.) Anyway, you could hear my sister's response about ten miles away: "They'll never stop talking about this. I'll be ninety years old, and the kids will still remind me how you embarrassed me tonight. You always embarrass me. *I hate you!*"

My dad just responded, "That's okay, honey, but we're going home." Then he went up to the boy and said (let's skip the first few words), "If you drive like that in front of me, with my little girl in the car, there is no way in the world I will let you out of my sight. I've got seventeen years invested in her, and you've only known her for one. No, sir. If that's the way you drive, you will *not* have her in your car."

Well, we didn't talk about it much that evening, or even at the breakfast table the next day; in fact to this day we don't say a lot about it. But I'll never forget two Christmases ago, when my sister and her family were about to embark on a beautiful life of serving the Lord on the mission field. Nancy went up to my dad and said, loud enough so we all could hear, "Dad, do you remember the time. . . ? Thanks for loving me that much."

As parents we have to be that secure door. We have to stand on our principles. Teens really need adults like us to stand up and say, "Right is right and wrong is wrong, no matter how you label it. I don't care how you try to gloss over it; there will never be a right way to do a wrong thing."

I also remember what happened when my three older (and beautiful) sisters came home from a date and sat in the driveway for a while before coming into the house. It was fine with my mom and dad if they stayed in the car for as long as it took to turn off the ignition. After that, my mom became master of the light switch. On and off the outdoor light went as she flew up and down, on her tiptoes. She'd look out and ask my dad, "That's your daughter out there, what are you going to do about it? What do you think they're doing out there—homework?"

One father in the same situation said to his wife, "You know, mom, dads are meant to help, aren't they?"

"Yes," she replied.

Putting on his coat, the father said, "Then I'm going to go out there and *help them in*."

Once he got out there, his daughter asked, "Don't you trust me, daddy?"

"No!" he exclaimed. "I wouldn't even trust *me* out here under these circumstances. Get in the house."

Young people continually tell me they feel glad when mom or dad says they can't go here or do that or be with a particular group. Even though they might disagree at the time, in the long run they know that their parents love them and care enough to show it. Show your teens. It's not enough to tell them about right and wrong; give them some life lessons, too.

Eight

Have the Courage to Say No

T eens need to have parents who *will* say no—not all the time, of course, but when it's necessary. However, if you *do* say no, also have the courage to tell your teens *why* you said it. Don't just proclaim "Don't do drugs." Tell them why. Become informed and educated. (In less than an hour you can read the three chapters of my book for teens, *Tough Turf*, in which I talk about drugs. You can also seek out other books and articles that will give you information on the topic.) Explain the effects drugs have on lives. By using this ammunition, you can lead your children into a better understanding of their dangers.

Remember, though, you can't talk it if you don't walk it. Make sure your life reflects your *nos*.

Help Them Develop Good Habits

When I asked her about raising teens, my aunt Virginia told me of one of the latest crazes for younger teens: cruising the malls. (Now don't get me wrong, I have nothing against malls. It's all in the use you make of them.) For many young teens who are too young to get a driver's license, going to the malls to look for guys has become a favorite pastime. Usually a group of three to five girls will spot a good-looking guy and tail him, getting close enough for him to hear their comments, such as, "Boy, he's cute." "He sure would look good in that outfit." "What a hunk!" Or "I'd look great walking with him."

Many parents find it hard to identify with girls chasing guys this way, because they never would have done it when they were teens. However, until mom and dad can explain the reasons why cruising isn't a good idea, their teens will probably merely think of them as old fogeys. Perhaps their young poeple would listen better if they explained that:

1. It is unhealthy to get used to the sexual connotations and promiscuity that form a large part of such flirting. Despite many popular opinions to the contrary, promiscuity has devastating long-term effects.
2. Though cruising the malls may not seem that way to teens, too much idle and unproductive time leaves the door wide open for alcohol, drugs, sex, crime, and the like. Just look at the relationship between teens with a lot of idle time on their hands and the young people who get into trouble.
3. This kind of time use promotes laziness.

4. When a teen spends too much time alone at a mall, it
   opens up the possibility of a kidnapping or molestation.

Though your daughter may not agree with all you say in ex-
planation of the no, at least she will know that you've considered
her welfare and have done some thinking about her situation. In
the years to come, she may even thank you for helping her
develop some alternative, good habits that have lasted a lifetime.

Give Alternatives

In suggesting that you be the secure door, I do not mean to
imply that you have to become dictatorial with your teens—far
from it.

If you've set sixteen as the age at which you will let your
daughter double date, and she wants to do it one week short of
her sixteenth birthday, don't merely deny her the right to date—
give an alternative. Don't make her run away from home because
she feels you won't give in. Instead let her invite her friends to
your house for a pizza party. Pizza's practically a miracle invitation for most teens—if that doesn't work, it's nearly hopeless!
Make time spent in your home interesting for your teen and her
friends. Check out some of the clean videos available, rent them,
and let the young people watch them. Provide some fun activities
for them. Show them mom and dad are not just stuffy, but that
you care enough to let them have a good time, even in the midst
of the family.

Nine

Teens Need Their Parents to ...

Help Them Build on Solid Foundations

Some teens, like Harry, never seem to have someone to turn to and always seem to stumble and fall. Unlike most people, who make errors they can fix or walk away from, Harry always got into the worst trouble possible. He came from a broken home, and no one seemed to care much what he did or where he went. After a series of run-ins with school authorities, nights when he never came home, and other troubles, he had an experience that seemed to seal his future. One night he took his girl friend to a drive-in and became a bit overfriendly. At first Annie played along with him, but when it got too much, she cried rape. Even though things hadn't gone that far, Harry spent time in jail—before he reached his twenty-first birthday.

Have you taught your teens that not every mistake gives a second chance? Have you shown them that two young people who have sex before marriage may have a lot of other trouble, too—like the responsibility of having a child (or aborting it) before either of them can drive? Does your son know that if he drinks and drives he could run head-on into another car—killing a whole family? Stories like these may seem extreme, but they happen every year, in every neighborhood. Help your teens avoid such situations by helping them understand the risks their actions may carry with them.

In order to avoid errors like these, your young people must know they can build their lives on a better foundation than the latest craze or the "if it feels good, it is good" philosophy that prevails today. Give your teens somewhere to turn.

Four Foundation Blocks

The most popular book of all time—the Bible—describes the ideal teenager. In one sentence, the Apostle Luke penned His qualities: "And he [Jesus] grew in *wisdom* and *stature*, in favor with *God* and *man*" (Luke 2:52). These four elements describe our foundational points:

1. *Wisdom:* Each of us has *mental* capabilities.
2. *Stature.* We all are *physical* beings.
3. *God.* This refers to our *spiritual* being.
4. *Man.* We are all *social*, we each need others.

Let's look at the ways in which we as parents can grow with our teens and help them grow, too.

MENTAL.   If you read one book this year, you will be in the upper 5 percent of Americans. Grow mentally, read, change, turn off the TV, and play some games, use your imagination. Our mental muscles, like our physical ones, become flabby if we never give them exercise.

Get your mental muscles back into shape. You don't have to be an Einstein, just make use of what you have. Show your teens that you don't mind looking in the dictionary or encyclopedia if you don't know something. Help them learn where to find information they need.

One of the greatest joys you can give a teen is the love of reading. For years and years my mother tried to share that with me, but I didn't catch on. Finally, she did get through. Today when I read, I realize how much I can learn; I can walk with kings, learn how to build shelves, or fix something around the house (being a klutz with tools, I probably wouldn't do those last two, but it *is* possible). If my mother had not persisted, I would have missed hundreds of hours of pleasure. Thanks, mom, for the gift of a lifetime.

One of America's outstanding communicators, Charley Tremendous Jones, shared the method he used to help his son learn to love reading: He actually encouraged his son to read books by paying him ten dollars for every book he read. His son could put it toward his college education, a new automobile, or whatever he wished.

After his son completed each book, Charley would ask for a simple book report, telling the essence of the book, what his son had learned, and how he planned to put it into practice.

Charley said his son never earned enough money to buy a car, but he sure learned to love reading. (As I remember, he borrowed his dad's car and even had to pay for the gas.) One teen fortunate enough to have had parents who encouraged him to read said, "Today I love to read, and it is mostly because of the encouragement my parents gave me in my early years. Through the books I read, I have seen people who did things right and did things wrong. I have learned what to do and what not to do. I have also learned that through books I can gain knowledge in any field I choose."

PHYSICAL. We need food to live, but sometimes we just don't need as much of it as we'd like. If you ever go to the refrigerator and nothing seems to look good, that means something: You're not hungry. When that happens, take these simple steps:

1. Shut the door.
2. Take your hand off the handle.
3. Run (this is the hard part).

If we want to get the best from the bodies God has given us, we have to care for them. Read the labels of the food you eat, find out how much sugar, salt, and fat you consume each day. Don't go *on* diets; instead change your life-style and way of thinking so you won't have to go *off* them.

You don't have to keep up with or compete with your kids, but do lead the way in sensible eating and exercise habits. Walk instead of riding in a car. Take a stairway instead of an elevator. Don't grab the closest parking-lot space. Do some sit-ups or jump rope. Ride a bike. Make exercise a healthy habit you can share with your teens.

SPIRITUAL. When I give my seminars, I can often see the thoughts in peoples' minds as I come to this. Their eyes share, *I'd go to church, too, if there weren't so many hypocrites down there.* I love what one minister said to that: "You ought to come down; one more won't matter."

Some people say, "Bill, I'd go to church, too, but frankly I don't get anything out of it." I wish I could ask them to mine—we give out free bulletins!

Other folks complain that they don't read the Bible because they don't understand it. Mark Twain said, "It's not the parts about the Bible that I don't understand that bother me." If those people were honest, they probably would agree with that statement. God speaks clearly. I'll bet you've noticed that He didn't give Moses the Ten Suggestions!

Of the four legs on our foundational chair in life, the spiritual one is by far the most important, and it's one we must take advantage of in our parenting. The Creator of the universe has offered each of us His strength for every situation. Keeping a family glued together *with* God's help is tough enough. I can't imagine taking on that difficult, challenging task without having Him on your side. Use all the strength and power available to you through Him.

Ask Jesus Christ into your heart as your personal Savior. He died on the cross for each and every one of us. Whether or not you believe that, it's true. If you've never accepted Him as Savior, God is tugging at your heart, inviting you to know Him. You may ask Jesus to become your Savior by using this simple prayer.

> Dear Jesus, I realize that I am a sinner. I've goofed up so many times. I'm so sorry for all the sins I've committed and all the times I've hurt You and others. I also realize that in my sinful state, without Your forgiveness, I will not see eternal life. Without You, I will go to hell forever. Lord, I ask that as Your Word says, You will forgive my sins, cleanse me, and come into my heart as personal Lord and Savior. I realize that Your death on the cross has already paid the price for my sins. Come into my heart and take control of my life. Thank You now, Lord, for loving me.

If you have prayed that prayer and really meant it, you have just taken the most important and wonderful step in your life—

not only for yourself, but for your family. Write me (see page 154 for my address). I'd like to encourage you in your new faith. You now have the ability to share God's love and peace and power with others.

I can honestly say that the most important and wisest decision I have ever made took place on Christmas Day, 1978, when I asked Jesus into my heart. He has never left me, through the good and bad times. His Word, the Bible, has constantly provided strength and gratification; His promises in the Word give me the hope and guidelines to keep me going every day. As I stay close to His Word and in fellowship with others who believe in Him I rarely have a bad day.

When others ask me how I'm doing, I can truly say, "Better and better." "Great." "Fantastic." No matter how tough life seems, I always can realize that God has forgiven my past and future sins. In the present I walk with the Creator of the universe in my heart. I have a guaranteed future with Him. A mansion on streets of gold waits for me, in a day when I get to live for eternity with God and all the others who have believed in Him. Why should I have a bad day? As a Christian, I of all people have ample reasons for having every single day be a positive one.

If you prayed the prayer I gave earlier, please write me at the address in the back of the book. I have some materials I will send to you. Just tell me that you have accepted Jesus as your Savior and would like to continue growing in the spiritual area of your life. While you're waiting for the materials, read the New Testament and join a Bible study and a church where people study the Word of God.

SOCIAL. Each one of us is a social creature, and we need support for other people. Let's not forget that teens are people, too—we need them, and they need us. Though your young people need encouragement and popularity with their friends, the most important people they need those elements from are you, mom and dad.

The greatest social tip I can offer you on teens is this: *Be friends with your child's friends.* Make your home a happy place to visit, a place they can come to often.

Notice that I said to be *friends* with your teen—that means friends, not pals. Your teens don't want someone else to play video games with. They don't want or need you to dress like them. But they do need and want you to laugh with them, be creative, spontaneous, and try new things with them. If your home is a place where your child's peers visit often, you will: (1) know who your child's friends are and (2) be in a position to influence them all. Millions of parents wish they could do that, but they do not have homes the kids enjoy staying at. The price, shape, size, or location of your home does not matter. What does matter is the love, laughter, caring, and ability to listen that show through.

If the kids aren't coming over, don't forget the pizza. Also get some creative books on ideas for parties, fun, and excitement. Turn your house into a friendly place. Let me warn you though, that parents who try to do this through drugs and alcohol have done the worst thing possible. In many cases, the law makes them totally liable for any mishaps that result on the night or day after a party of that kind.

I've shared the four foundations of life with you, but I also know that many teens try to go through those tough years of life on just one leg. Some are all social—they talk, talk, talk. Others are mental—bookworms. A third kind are all spiritual—they read their Bibles all day.

The most popular person in the school frequently has only two legs. For the jock or superstar athlete, the social and physical legs are strong, but not the spiritual or mental. The beauty queen has the same problem. When even the "cream of the crop" has only two legs, what of the student who just doesn't fit in, isn't beautiful, or acts klutzy? No wonder our young people hurt. We should not feel surprise that the number-one problem in college is depression, and the number-two killer in high school is suicide.

Kids desperately need to feel a part of something, someone, or some group. That's why, in the beginning of the school year, the football or basketball coach quite often has the most power in the school, as far as kids are concerned. He's got them coming home before curfew, getting homework done, and staying off drugs and alcohol. As a part of a team, each member has to be there, because others count on him. He has to meet the eligibility requirements—and he knows it.

Families need the same attitude. Count on your children. They want to be depended on and to have something to live up to. Former football great Bill Glass, who has a number of prison ministries across the country, reports that when they were young, 95 percent of the men and women in prison today were repeatedly told by an authority figure that they would grow up to go to jail. Others expected them to live up to that, and they did.

When was the last time you caught your son or daughter, red-handed, doing something positive? I mean *caught* him or her—made a big deal of it, telling everyone whom you talked to, writing friends and relatives. What would happen in our schools if, every time a student was caught doing something positive, he got some kind of encouragement? Teens would look for special ways to be noticed and appreciated, and that's all they really want anyway.

Help your child build his or her life on the right foundations. Then keep encouraging!

Ten

Teens Need Their Parents to . . .

Help Them Find Their Special Talent

Your teens need to know that they can be good at something. In school, students constantly compare themselves with others, but usually in a way that will only hurt them or tear them down. A boy looks at another and says to himself, *He's a terrific athlete. I'm so clumsy. I couldn't do that well, even if I got on the team.* Or a girl thinks, *Patty's the most beautiful girl in the class. All the boys like her, but I can't even get a date.* When teens try to measure up in terms of unchangeable things—like contrasting themselves to someone else's looks, talents, or family—they will always fall short. If your teens must compare, teach them to do so against skills they can also learn well and excel in. If your son's not athletic, don't encourage him to compare himself to a football star. Maybe he's a better student than that boy or has artistic talent he should develop. Help him to make the most of his best points. This is called positive comparison.

79

In order to hold their heads high and feel proud of themselves when they walk through the school halls, young people need to be known for something. Not all students can be the prettiest, most popular, best on the football field, or most intelligent. But each teen has a talent that can help him or her stand out in a positive way, and we need to help every boy or girl find that, or he or she will stand out in a negative way—by supplying dope to other teens, acting up in class, or talking more loudly than anyone else—to get attention.

When I was in high school, I desperately needed to stand out somehow. It took me a while to find my talent, but one day I learned I was good at business. I earned money in the summertime, with my friend Steve, by traveling around the United States, painting yellow lines on parking lots. When I came back to school in the fall, with my new car and a healthy bank account, people started noticing me. I had a special talent: I could run a business as well as or better than 90 percent of all the students in my school. I was the only senior who had his own business, his own car, and employees working for him. Ever since then, that talent has played a major role in my life, because it was an early way for me to receive positive recognition.

You Can't Do Everything Well

As you help your teen find his or her special talent, also show your son or daughter that one cannot be good at everything. As I studied this, I noticed that most people are good at four or five things, at the most. Take me for example. My spiritual walk with God is the most important area in my life, so I spend regular time thinking about, talking to, and listening to God. Being a father and a husband, having a secure family, comes next. I work hard at it and put time in at it, so I have a successful family. My speaking career is also very important to me. Because I spend many hours working at it, I rate fairly well at that. In addition, I love the game of golf, but I only get to play it once (at the most twice) a week—except in the spring, when I get carried away. In order for me to vastly improve my golf score, the game would have to maintain a high importance level in my life, which means I would have to spend much more time at it. (Notice that the two key factors in developing a special talent are *importance* and *time*.) However, if I tried to make golf a real priority in my life, my family or career would probably suffer. I would have to take time away from those to improve my score. It just isn't worth it to me, because my family and career are too important. All that means is that I'll never be another Arnold Palmer.

While you encourage your teen to develop a talent, also help him or her maintain a high level of self-confidence and a healthy self-esteem, even when performance in a certain area is down. The teen who comes home after being rejected for the baseball team probably suffers from low self-esteem, and that may affect all areas of his life. He's likely to see himself not only as a failure on the baseball field, but at everything from his grades to his homelife. Show him it's not true and explain that everyone can't do everything. We are all lousy at something. Point out a few people—perhaps some of his heroes—who have great talents in one area, but not another.

Don't Raise Quitters

If your teen discovers a talent, don't let her start it and immediately give it up. It takes time to become good at anything—time and practice. When I asked about this, one parent shared that she had a son who wanted to play the trumpet. From past experience.

she was fairly sure her son would lose interest after a while. The family did not have a lot of money to buy a horn that would be laid aside in a few weeks or months, so they decided to contract—that's right, they actually wrote out a contract—that the son would play the trumpet for two years, if his parents bought it.

In taking this up, the son agreed to spend regular time practicing the instrument, take care of it, and participate in the band or other school functions, including tryouts and auditions.

Once they had contracted all this, the parents bought the trumpet, and the boy began the lessons with great eagerness and excitement. However, not far down the road, the son, being a creature of habit, decided playing the trumpet was old hat, hard work, and no longer thrilling. He went to his parents and asked if he could quit the lessons.

Tactfully his parents reminded him, "When you started this, you signed a contract that said you'd do it faithfully for two years." Mention of the contract worked like magic. At first the son hemmed and hawed and tried to give the gift that keeps on giving: guilt. In the end, parents and son sat down and cried together, but they ended up agreeing that the contract had not been fulfilled. As people of their word, they owed it to themselves not to become quitters.

A few months later the son had braces put on and tried to end the contract. "This looks as if you're trying to find a way out again," mom and dad commented. Instead, together they discovered a way that he could play, using more of his lip. He continued to play the trumpet.

What a valuable experience these parents gave their son. Many times, throughout the rest of his teen years and post-high-school years, in college and the working world, or in the early years of marriage, their son would have many opportunities to quit. But when he looked back at this, he would see another resource, one that gave him more stickability and reason to believe he could follow through on any project. All this resulted from the actions of a mom and dad who cared enough to work full time at parenting and use some practical techniques to teach their son a valuable life lesson.

Teach your children the same lesson by helping them stick through the tough parts of any learning situation. (Turn to the Appendix for more information on contracts, if you want to try one.) Naturally if your daughter wants to learn to sing and then finds out she's tone deaf, you would discontinue the lessons. If your son starts doing woodworking and discovers that he's so hopelessly clumsy that it's no use, after a while you might let him stop. But in most cases your teens will feel attracted to areas in which they may learn to achieve, and it's worthwhile to continue. Don't let your young people quit too soon. They need to experience success!

Eleven

Give Them Quality and Quantity Time

One woman shared with me how she bought a beautiful dinette set. When she found it at a garage sale, the chairs and table were covered with paint and food stains from years on end, and it had a very marred finish. After paying a few dollars for it, she took the set home, cleaned it up, refinished it, and ended up with some very expensive furniture.

Later she found that a friend had bought an identical set at an expensive antique auction and paid about twenty times as much for the very same thing. Five dollars at a garage sale, plus some time and quite a lot of fun or one hundred dollars at an expensive auction equaled the same thing.

In buying furniture, the expensive but quick method the second woman used might seem (and be) more painless, but don't try it when it comes to raising your teens. Through money you cannot buy love and affection or give the priceless gift of memories. You simply *have* to spend time with people to have that kind of relationship. A few dollars spent on activities that take several hours always get better results than spending thousands on your son or daughter, in the hope that it will take the place of time and fun.

To make your children happy, you do not have to spend extravagantly or give them the biggest and the best. In fact, the simpler, the better. Recently I saw a television show that featured interviews with young people from a rich suburb of Dallas, Texas. These teenagers said that when they grew up, they wanted to move away from the area and go to a place where people don't have to travel or move if the company says to; where the people aren't plastic, but real; where looks aren't as important as feelings; where automobiles and fancy boats don't count more than true friendships. They'd seen through all their world had to offer and wanted to get back to a simpler way of life.

Time and Importance

We spend time in those areas of our life that are most important to us personally. That's an important concept, and our teens have picked up on it. They might as well have put it in a formula like this:

Time spent = interest = commitment = love

Perhaps they just sense that parents who love them spend time with them.

QUALITY VERSUS QUANTITY. The statement "quality time is much better than quantity time" is for the birds. Your child, just like your spouse, needs a lot of your time. When you shortchange your teen, you shortchange yourself.

Take your favorite food, for example. When it comes to that

area, we all definitely like quality. But if you could only have one bite of your favorite food, without quantity, would its quality still please you? I doubt it. You wouldn't agree that quality food is better than quantity food—especially if you were starving!

In a way the fast-food mentality represents what some American teens get from their parents as well. Mom or dad wants the same quality, but quicker service, faster times together—"I'll take the hamburger now, instead of in ten minutes. Even though it won't be fresh off the grill, that's okay, because I have an important appointment a few minutes from now." Fast-food parenting doesn't have a lot of benefits.

Those young people really want mom and dad to show them that in the same way the time of that appointment has importance, so does time set aside for *them*. Teens know that love shown by parents says, "Your life is important, daughter [or son], and I'm going to give you my time." When you spend time with them, show them you will listen and talk and work things out together.

Gifted speaker Dr. James Kern shares the story of a little boy who wanted to build a tree house with his father, but night after night, for two or three weeks, the dad forgot and came home from work too late.

Finally the dad remembered one morning and said to his son, "Tonight's the night." He told his boy to come home right after school, and dad would meet him there. They would go get the lumber and make the tree house. As Jim says, "Guess what young person didn't learn a thing all day in school? You've got it. That little boy." All he thought about was, *Tonight my daddy and I are going to build that tree house together.* He ran all the way home from school—right into the path of an oncoming vehicle. Just one word described his condition in the hospital: *coma.*

His mom and dad rushed to the hospital, and several hours later the little boy opened his eyes, to say his final words to his father: "Daddy, you won't have to build that tree house." Then that little boy went away. Now the father is going through a severe depression, has lost a lot of weight, and quit his job, all because he could have shared (but didn't know) five of the most valuable words in the world, when it comes to spending time with a son or daughter: *How long will it take?*

I've tried those words on my four-year-old daughter, Emily. When I ask, she almost always says something like, "Five minutes, daddy." "Just one more story." "Two more times around the block." When she was three and a half, I tried this, but I learned her idea of time was a lot different from mine. She wanted me to read a story and answered my question, "Just seven years, daddy."

DON'T WAIT!   We usually meet our child's needs a lot better if we meet them right away. When a young person needs help, guess when he or she needs it? *Right away!* At plenty of the student and youth functions where I speak, right after my talk, many hurting young people line up, waiting to speak to me, because they don't know where to turn. They ask what I think of certain things or they want my advice or they just plain need help. Quite often I miss my next session because we have to deal with their problems then and there. I've also felt gladdened to see the sensitivity of educators around the country, men and women who realize the importance of the moment and can carry on with a problem shared by a student just as if that were the way things were meant to be.

Did you know that if I spend extra time with a student, it sometimes messes up a flight schedule? Big-shot speaker that I am, I have an agreement with the airlines. It's a simple one: If they are ready to go, and I'm not there—they can! Guess what? They do.

Take Time to Care

In dealing with teens' hurts and problems, we can have a difficult time, because if they feel we don't want to know or don't truly care or don't have the time, they won't tell us what bothers them. But even if a teen doesn't say it in words, his attitude can give you a clue. If the expression on her face gives you the impression your daughter wants to share, or if your son just becomes silent for a while, make the first effort to communicate. If she drops a hint at the dinner table, please suggest that you go somewhere quiet for a talk, after you've eaten. Make sure you'll have no interruptions, like the TV, phone, family, or friends.

Once you get alone with your teen, just ask what's wrong and how you can help. Find out what the problem is. If your child does not want to share, tell her you will talk later, when she feels more comfortable. You have already taken the most important step, by showing you care and will be there.

However, don't say you care once and expect your teen to share every trouble with you. Keep asking over and over again, if necessary, to encourage your son or daughter to tell you of the hurts and joys. Your teen has something called pride, and you'll need to break that barrier. Turning into an adult is awfully scary, but teens have a hard time admitting it. In addition your son or daughter has seen the hypocrisy of the world, which tells them that parents think, *No kids will hold me back. I've got a career to run. Don't you know I'm too busy to bother with teens' troubles?* They've seen parents act as if they thought this way and need to know you are different and really care. They'll only know it if you show them. Do that!

Twelve

Teens Need Their Parents to . . .

Show Affection and Give Hugs

Even if your son squirms away every time you try to touch him or your daughter sidles from the room when you praise her, your teens need to feel and hear affection. Though they may seem uncomfortable at first, they need the looks, words, or gestures that show you care: a simple hug, a hand on the shoulder, a pat on the back, or words that show your pride in them—when you talk to them and about them.

A Touch of Love

Some parents may wonder, *How can I show affection? I just wouldn't know where to begin. Anyway, if I went all goofy over my kids, they'd know I was faking it.* Chances are that some of those parents have sons who wrestle with them, headlocks and the whole bit, crying out for affection and desperate for dad's physical touch. Other parents may think, *That's just not the way I am. My mom and dad didn't do that, and I turned out okay.* But hugging is a habit you, too, could come to enjoy.

One girl described physical affection in her family this way: "I know mom and dad loved us all a lot, but in my family, it seemed as if everyone was surrounded by a safety zone—we very rarely did much hugging or touching. Only after I became a Christian and started going to a church where people hugged a lot could I feel comfortable hugging my parents. I had to start the habit in my family, but now everyone really enjoys it. I've been hugging them for a few years now—several times a day—and they really like it. In fact sometimes they want more hugs than I do!"

Don't wait for your teens to start the affection habit. The first few times you try may seem difficult, but they'll soon pick up on it, if you really mean it.

One parent said, "I give kids pats on the back, low and hard, whenever they goof up," but I'm not talking about that. It's not really affection, it's discipline. Kids today need the comfort of a touch—and should know that it's okay to cry (even if you are a boy). Instead we've taught our children, "Big boys, [or girls] don't cry," and they've learned the lesson well. Because they've learned that attitude, it's not surprising teens have a hard time opening themselves up to feelings—especially the hurting ones. Why haven't we stood up and told our young people that big boys and girls *do* cry and *ought* to cry, because those who do live longer and cope with life better? Teach your teens to show their affection—and not be afraid to express pain.

Words Show Affection, Too

Every day, use words to show love to your teens. Praise them when they do something wonderful or make their goals. Let them know how you feel inside. When they become adults, your example will give them the same ability to share support for others, because they learned it well from you.

One word of warning, though. If you have a number of children, be certain you encourage them all—and fairly equally. Nothing feels worse for younger brother John than to continually hear, "Pete does so well in school. He always gets straight A's," when John just got a D in English. Let John know that he achieves in some things Pete can't do, or the hurt of those A's could influence his relationship with his brother. That pain may also encourage John to rebel, just to get some attention of his own.

Also, be sure you let the teen you appreciate know it. Don't just tell John how wonderful Pete's grades were—tell *Pete* how you feel, too. After all, that's the point of all the praise, isn't it?

Thirteen

Teens Need Their Parents to . . .

Brag about Them

When I speak to teens, they often say, "My dad brags on me," or, "I wish my parents *would* brag on me," and you can see the truth of either message in those teens' eyes. If a guy has parents who feel proud of him, he can do almost anything, in his own mind. If a girl has parents who think she's no good, it's as if nothing could help. *I'm a loser,* she'll decide. *Why even try?*

Your teens don't have to become losers, if you encourage them by bragging on them—to their faces and behind their backs.

Two women I knew couldn't have been more different when it came to talking about their children. The first often spoke of her sons in an honest but positive way. Though she knew they weren't perfect (nobody is), she always had a good word to say about their latest accomplishments. Everyone in her family and at work knew how wonderful she thought they were. Her straightforward approach to them was refreshing, not overpowering at all.

The second mother had nothing but harsh words for her daughters. Now that they were grown, they never came to visit her. Before the eyes of the world she laid out every flaw she could find, for public inspection. Not too many people cared to listen to her when she began to tell of each child's latest failings. Perhaps they knew why the daughters never kept in touch.

Of those children, which would you rather be? Which kind of parent would you rather be?

When you talk to and about your teens, remember that what you say could turn their lives around. Doug English, one of the most respected NFL players, and I met in the locker room a couple of years ago. I will never forget his response when I asked this great football player, "How did you grow up positive, and how do you stay positive?" He said:

1. His parents always loved each other, and they made it apparent to their children that they would always be together.
2. His was raised in the church, as a family.
3. His parents always bragged on him.

When I asked him why it was so important for his mom and dad to have built him up, he said he didn't become a superstar in football for a long time. If not for his parents building him up and his coaches spending extra time with him, he probably wouldn't have made it at all. Notice where the spark began: His parents bragged on him. They talked positively to and about their son.

I know what he means, because I've got to confess that the greatest thing my parents did for me (besides raising me in the church) was to never stop believing in me. They always stayed behind me, in everything I did. No matter how many ideas I had, they never condemned any of them—not even the terrible ones.

I continually felt my parents loved me. *They are proud of me,* I thought, *and with them believing in me I don't care if others don't.*

Show your teens you believe in them. It works: In fact, it has an extra benefit you've probably never thought of: motivation.

Motivate Your Teens

For years I've heard parents complain, "I can't motivate my children." Then they ask me, "How should I do it?" When it comes to this subject, I have what I call the Butterfly Theory: If you forget about motivating your children and concentrate on something else, the motivation will come naturally.

Most people who want to catch a butterfly take a net and start chasing around after the butterfly. But everyone knows butterflies move faster than nets—nets can't even fly! The secret to catching a butterfly is to find an old mud hole, sit on a rock next to it, and hold perfectly still, while you count your blessings. As you start to give thought to who sent the sunshine that day, lo and behold, butterflies land all over you. They are so beautiful and close that you don't even need to catch them and take them home with you.

The same principle holds true with your son and daughter, when it comes to motivation. Take your eyes off the motivation, and you can use the PAM method:

Perception + Attitude = Motivation

Notice that perception and attitude come before motivation. As you help give your sons and daughters the perception that they are winners, that they are honest and good, can handle their problems, and can make the team, their attitude takes care of itself, and motivation comes as a natural follow-up.

If you repeatedly tell your teen he's a loser and will only end up in jail, he probably will. That's all you've given him to work with in his mind, and repeated comments such as those will instill that message in his mind. Even if it's not true, your words will work to kill that young man's motivation.

At the same time, positive reinforcement will make your teen a winner. Look at the perception of any highly motivated young person in your neighborhood. She thinks she's a good kid, that she is capable, can handle things, that people like her, and so on.

In order to motivate Emily, I don't try to get her to be popular with the kids. Instead I try to give her the perception that she *is* popular and well-liked.

I do this by feeding her short sentences like:

> *"People always like you."*
> *"It's funny, but you keep getting more friends every day."*
> *"Do you notice how people smile when they're around you?"*
> *"I'm so happy at the way you make people feel good about themselves."*
> *"You sure are a happy girl today!"*
> *"Good morning, Emily, I bet you expect a good day today, don't you?"*

Now she expects such comments and has begun to come back with some of her own, like:

> *"Today is a good day, isn't it, dad?"*
> *"Hey, dad, let's go have a good day."*
> *"Dad, my friends sure are happy. Did you see them?"*

I even noticed that one day, when she'd come home after a fight with her friends, she hadn't complained about it. I asked what happened, and she told me, "Oh, it'll be better tomorrow. They are still my friends."

Work on your teen's perception. Attitude will follow, and the motivation will appear all on its own. (Remember PAM and don't forget the butterflies.) But also keep in mind that you can't improve someone's perception overnight. It takes short bits of information over a long period of time to make that change. Stick to realistic, small goals at first, because giant leaps won't happen.

Picture your mind as a cassette with four miles of tape on it. Let's compare that to the length of a lifetime. If your son or daughter has ten or twelve years of tape with only minimal positive instructions, it will take a while for the new way of thinking to take hold.

It's like starting a weight-loss or exercise program. You don't reach your goal overnight. When people treat those programs in the wrong way, they become short-term Band-Aids, instead of life-style changes. Many people "go on" diets, only to "go off" them because they haven't had a major alteration in attitude. To help your teen develop a positive mind-set, you need to make a life-style change—for both of you. You'll need to remember to say the good things, and your teen will have to learn to think them about himself or herself.

Take the time to say something kind—it could change both your lives. But remember, you have to make a habit of it!

Fourteen

Teens Need Their Parents to . . .

Learn More about Them and Their Friends

Teens today don't have the same way of doing things, the same music, and the same language they had when you or I were that age. Each new generation has its own way of defining what's cool and what's not, and as parents, it's up to us to do our homework and find out more about our children's world: What drugs are being sold in our communities, whether alcohol or marijuana is the bigger problem in the local schools, what teens use as the latest term to put down others, how easily a seventeen-year-old can enter a bar and get served, what parts of town never get checked for drunk drivers, and so on.

For years your sons and daughters have asked me to inform you that you've got to learn a little more about what goes on with today's teenagers' world. Unless you do this, you can't adequately identify with them.

One way to find out more is to talk to your teens and their

friends. Read a little bit to learn about the most common drugs. Listen to the popular music for their age group, to discover what kind of lyrics they hear all the time. Ask why they won't go to church or stay home with the family. What do they feel ashamed about? Why does being seen with mom and dad in public seem one of the worst offenses they could commit?

Just as the owner of a department store has to keep up with the changing needs of his customers, parents need to keep up with developments in their teens' lives. By finding out what goes on in their world, parents can reach them and love them and identify with them. Don't feel that you have to act as they do or talk like them in order to listen or express interest. Teens today, more than ever, have an interest in stability, going back to the basics, using old-fashioned ideas, returning to the fundamentals. Share your beliefs with them, in a new, creative way. They really are waiting: Like the trend in ties, which moves from wide to narrow to wide, people change in attitudes. In the past thirty years, things have gone so far that now teens are desperately trying to get back to the basics of family life.

Recently I talked to one sixteen-year-old who had gotten a buzz cut a few months before. When people saw his nearly bald head, they stared and thought he looked strange. "How did your parents react to it?" I asked. "They didn't," he told me. At least they didn't react the way most parents would. Although they didn't feel that great about it, they let him be himself. They kept a sense of humor about the situation, and now they are best of friends with their son. One day, in church, I saw his mother joking with him, and it was apparent they had a beautiful relationship.

I couldn't help but ask him *why* he shaved his head. "Hardly anyone ever asked me that," he replied. "They just assumed I was weird. I did it for the swimming team I was on." It's easy for adults to look at a teen and *assume*. Don't let that sort of rash judgment spoil your relationship with your son or daughter. Discover the facts, first.

Even if it's something bigger than the length of a child's hair, don't cut off communication with your daughter or son. Instead look at the big picture. One day your child will grow out of this stage. Someday your daughter may be the mother of your grandchild. You may need to depend on your son, when you're older. Don't let differences in culture build a wall between you and your teen, all because emotions got the best of you.

Remember: *If two people always agree, one of them isn't needed.*

Fifteen

Teens Need Their Parents to . . .

Let Them Do Things for Themselves

In today's world we place so much emphasis on success that sometimes we forget that it takes failures—the practice runs that teach us a skill or develop an ability—to make success. When it comes to your teens, allow them to make those mistakes, because only through the failures will they learn the skills they'll need as adults.

Your son or daughter wants to try things personally. Even if you think your son will goof up when he tries to change the oil in the lawnmower, let him help. Remember, you have twenty-five years' experience at the job, and he has none. How did you learn? By spilling the oil—so let him do that, too. A few drops of it are not the most important thing in the world.

Emily and I have a little saying: "Don't sweat the small stuff—it's *all* small stuff." Certainly we need to feel concern about some things in life, but have you ever thought about how many things are really small stuff? Don't get frantic and worried when your daughter doesn't come up with a Gucci outfit on her first sewing project—she'll improve with time. Let her learn by practice.

Hold to these guidelines as your teen learns something new:

1. Let her do it alone.
2. Remember: It's okay to fail.
3. Don't jump in and do it for her. Instead give a suggestion, to point your child in the right direction. If you give her the perception that you will jump in, that you won't let her do it anyway or you can't even let her try, your child won't want to develop a skill, much less have the motivation to try it.

Make the Most of Failure

When Emily was two, we told her about the hot flame on the stove or candle. "Don't touch that, or you will burn your fingers," I warned her, but I also let her do it anyway. When a child tries to touch the flame, most parents grab the little guy's hand, shove it back, and tell him not to do that. In fact, the best thing they could do is to let the child fail and touch the flame. As soon as he does it, he will think, *My mama don't lie!* (Don't use this method to teach a child to stay out of the road, though.)

From childhood we've all had to fall and scrape our knees, goof up here and there—and learn it's okay not to be perfect. In order to enter adulthood, we need to understand that failure is a perfectly normal part of life and has great teaching value. Make the most of that knowledge with your teens.

One young man shared the wisdom his parents showed during this part of his life: "All through my teen years, I remember how I would rush to do this or that or hurry into an activity. My mom and dad both could see clearly that I was going to stub my toe or run head on into a difficulty. They would just sit back and let me experience it by myself, but always seemed to be there to help pick me up and share a lesson. They never made me feel insignificant for goofing up.

"I was on the wrestling team at school, and in order to cut weight, I had to practically starve myself a couple of days before. I made the weight okay, but afterwards I got very sick. In my junior year of high school, I noticed that I wasn't growing very well. My parents noticed it, too. Instead of totally condemning the sport, as I probably would have if my child's growth was affected by it, they helped me see that I had other talents in areas of football and gymnastics, where I didn't have to starve myself during these special growing years. They loved me into other sports.

"They never told me, 'I told you so,' or asked, 'How come you belong to such a crazy activity?' They were just always there and always supporting.

"If I went on a camping trip and forgot my tent or lantern, they would let me forget it and learn to live with it and prepare better the next time. I just remember that while they let me grow, they never said, 'I told you so.' "

A Significant Difference

As I interviewed literally hundreds of people, in putting this book together, I learned again and again that the little things make the big difference in life. When I asked people in their twenties and thirties, "What did your parents do that made a significant difference in your life?" *never* did they say they appreciated the fact that mom and dad bought them whatever they wanted or did everything for them. In fact, their comments showed they most appreciated ways in which their parents had shaped their lives by letting them take on responsibility. Not one said, "They made life easy for me, and it has helped significantly."

Instead, I found that young people appreciate the actions their parents took that have made life realistic. When mom and dad have shown a daughter or son that certain consequences result from the way we structure our lives, that child has learned a valuable lesson. When parents have gently pushed and pulled their teens, sprinkling their direction-giving with love, it has shaped youngsters more than letting them drift aimlessly.

What steps can parents take to make that difference? Try these.

DISPEL FANTASIES.   Many young adults I spoke to told me they appreciated the fact that parents showed them life was not a fantasy. As tiny tots we think the toy in the cereal box will be as big, bright, and durable as it seemed on TV, but when that fragile, insignificant piece of plastic shatters the first time we play with it, we start to learn this lesson in life. Teach your teens the same thing.

Young people share that they wish parents wouldn't let them get away with things—like not finishing a chore or cleaning their rooms or doing their homework. Looking back on his teen years, John shared the principle of "help me out, but don't bail me out": "It seems that whenever I had a term paper or a special project to do, I could tell my mom, and she would do the typing. She would also do much of my homework for me.

"At the time, I enjoyed it, because I could wait until the last minute and still get my paper done or get a fairly good grade on the test the next day. However, I never learned the importance of doing things for myself or thinking ahead of time of what must be done.

"I think it is great to help your kids out, but *don't always bail them out* when they have a problem or need money or have a take-home test to do. It would have been better if I had learned how to type myself and taken care of my own responsibilities.

"As I look back, I thank my parents for loving me, but I wish they had encouraged me to do my own homework more often."

Instead show your teens, through your expectations and reactions, that life is real. Encourage them to learn that reality hurts, feels lonely, cries, laughs, and gets put down. It includes all the emotions life has to offer—both happy and sad. Help dispel the "life can be perfect" myth.

TEACH YOUR TEEN THAT LIFE HAS CONSEQUENCES. Recently I spoke to Fred, a man in his thirties, who commented that the greatest thing his father did for him was the thing he hated most at the time. Fred grew up on a farm, and his dad continually made him do chores. That alone doesn't seem unusual, but Fred's father also *expected* him to do a good job and *inspected* the job to see that his son had done it properly.

If Fred had not done a chore properly, his father made him do it again. It didn't matter if all Fred's friends had invited him to play in a ball game or to be part of another outing, and dad didn't accept excuses on Friday nights or Saturday mornings. If the job was not well-done, Fred would do it again. "After a while, I realized I might as well do the very best job possible, because I was going to have to do it over. There was no getting away from it," Fred commented.

Fred's dad gave him one of life's greatest gifts when he taught him that:

Life has consequences:
Our actions bring about reactions.

Letting a child go through life thinking that a sloppy job will be accepted by employers and the world sets him up for a rude awakening, failure, and heartaches.

Fred went on to say that he would often do an immaculate job of sweeping the barn, for instance. He cleaned out the cracks, crevices, and cobwebs, to make it look better than ever before. When he was nineteen, living on his own, far from home, doing a hard job in the heat of the summer, trying to make it on his own, he realized the value of those lessons. His father had given him the gift of taking pride in his work and doing a good job. Although he could have tried giving up and going home to mom and dad that summer, instead he called home to thank them for that gift. He said the perseverance they had taught him gave him the stickability and character to hang in there when times got tough. Today he looks back and credits much of his success in life to that well-taught early lesson.

MONEY NEEDS MANAGEMENT.   Looking back over their teen years, many people have told me that they most disliked the fact that their parents always gave them money whenever they asked for it. Those who felt this way shared that it can turn a person into a magnificent manipulator. They didn't have a hard time talking mom or dad into giving them money for something they wanted at that instant. But looking back, they realize such spur-of-the-moment purchases were almost always bad ones.

Getting all the money they wanted turned them into the sort of people who never thought about what they bought, looked ahead, or used sound judgment. They turned into impulse buyers. For example, one boy had two friends who had just bought ten-speed bicycles. Though his family did not have as much money as the others, he, too, just had to own one—and that week. Although he realized it would create a financial burden for his parents, he thought they wanted it that way, since whenever he cried, pouted, or put up a fuss, they never hesitated to give in.

After some arguing the parents bought him the bicycle, but later he said he never appreciated it and many times wished they had said no, because he felt he was part of their financial problems. In addition, for years he has struggled to overcome this idea that he can just buy anything whenever he wants to. Now he realizes he must think things over, earn the money, and understand that he has to sacrifice one item if he buys another. Basically, he has to become more responsible with his life.

Others have shared that they gave no thought to starting a savings plan, because they said to themselves, *Why spend my own money, since I can always get money out of mom and dad for this or that? I'll start saving another day.*

As parents we need to set down certain policies in dealing with money (and on other issues in our children's lives). Develop a plan while your son or daughter is in the early teen years, so he or she will know what to expect. Be flexible when necessary, but also have a stated guideline that influences most decisions.

I'm a big believer in the idea that parents should not cosign a loan for a teen's first car. If she has not learned the art of work, or if he has not learned to save, I don't believe a person deserves a car that is financially out of reach. In such a case, encourage your teen to buy a less expensive car with the money available.

Often I've heard of teens who have wrecked an automobile, leaving mom and dad with the bill. Because of the bitter feelings that resulted in many such incidents, it takes years for the relationships involved to get back in order. In addition, the teen has never learned the art of saving, and mom and dad remain stuck with repaying a loan they should never have given in the first place.

During the past fifty years, our young people have missed the privilege of doing without. We all need to learn that it is okay—and even emotionally healthy—not to get everything we want. When we have learned that lesson, we know that life does not always give us every desire, that we can stand up under pressures, and can enjoy ourselves in tough situations. Let your teen discover this at home, before he goes out into the world.

Naturally the family works as a team, and at times you may find it appropriate to lend money for a good reason. However, it must always be understood that the borrower will repay the money.

One fellow shared the money policy his parents had made. If he wanted a toy, he had to earn enough money to pay half the price. He said it taught him many things:

1. How to earn money.
2. How to save.
3. How to choose long-lasting items.
4. How to appreciate the sacrifices his parents made when they bought him something.

One young woman shared that she disliked the fact that when it came to money, her parents never related specifics to her and only talked in general. For instance, her dad would say, "Money doesn't grow on trees, you know," but he never encouraged her to start a bank account and save or showed her how to balance a checkbook. Until she lived alone, she never knew what it meant to budget for regular expenses.

Help your children tie the general to the specific. Give them concrete examples of how they can start paying their own bills.

SHOW TEENS THE VALUE OF COMMITMENT. Has your son or daughter wanted to sell something door-to-door—like candy, newspapers, magazines, or cookies? An experience such as this can turn into parent-child frustration or parent-child intimacy, depending on how you handle it.

One parent shared that his teen wanted to sell candy door-to-door. Before she got started, he sat down with her and asked, "Do you want to be a winner? Do you want to do this in a mediocre way or really stand out in your class?"

Once he got her commitment, he helped her visualize what it would feel like to be one of the very top salespeople in the school. Together they took a deep interest in the project and got the sales material. Then the father helped, drilled, and reinforced the sales presentation with his teen. He demanded excellence, not perfection. He kept the vision of her being a winner before her. He never gave her the impression, *I love you if you make it, but I won't if you don't.* Instead he implied, *You are capable of being a winner, and now that you have that vision in your mind, merely learn this presentation. Give it with enthusiasm, as many times as you can. If you work harder than anyone else, most likely you will be among the top winners.* She went on to do well in that project and the rest of her life. The key ingredient was the extra interest her father showed.

Notice the father did not do the job for his teen. Instead he inspired her and gave her the perception that she could win. Once she had started to believe she could achieve, she repeated that pattern over and over again.

Even if you have not had an experience of winning, you can paint such a picture of it in your mind that, even though you haven't done it, you can see it with such color and detail that it seems as if you had achieved it many times before. The attitude that fosters leads to real success.

START BUILDING CHARACTER, NOT WORLD WAR III.   How many times has everyone in a family lost his or her appetite because, five minutes before dinner, dad began screaming through the house, "Who took my screwdriver out of my toolbox and didn't return it?"

Growing up, I remember it was the easiest thing in the world to take a tool out of dad's toolbox, lay it down somewhere, and forget about it; it also pretty certainly started an argument. Haven't you talked to a parent who has gotten angry over that—or has even gotten to the point where he guards his tools with his very life?

One father shared his solution to the problem. His technique builds character and provides teens with a useful lifelong skill.

You're probably familiar with the instructions on most toys and projects—the ones that say a five-year-old can put it together. The problem with such kits is that they include everything but the five-year-old! My theory on it goes like this: At one time in the production of this toy, the company hired a five-year-old genius, who actually did put it together (with *only* the aid of six committees, four outside engineers, and the entire work force of the company!)

Well, this father came by his idea quite by accident one holiday season. Instead of building the toys or putting them together Christmas Eve, he waited until Christmas morning and had the kids help him with the task.

His youngsters not only learned how to put toys together, they also learned the use of and appreciation of tools, how to work with their hands, how to read instructions, how to think ahead, how to tear something apart if they made a mistake—and they also knew the value of their toys. If the screws were just plastic, they wouldn't abuse the toy as much, because they knew it would break.

Dad left his tools in a special place, unlocked, so his kids could share them. Soon they wanted their own, so they could care for them themselves, keep them clean, oiled, and polished, and use them whenever they wished.

His daughter took her toolbox to college and had the easiest and most unique way of meeting boys. The men on campus soon found out she was handy at that and would come by to ask for help or to borrow her tools. In addition she got a reputation as the only girl in the dorm who could do everything from hanging a bookshelf to fixing her own car.

When his sons went to find a job, they went with toolbox in hand. As they asked for an interview, they told a prospective boss, "If you hire me, you not only get someone who can run a cash register or sweep floors [or whatever the job]. You also get someone who comes with his tools. If something breaks while I'm on the job, I'm really adept at fixing it, and you won't have to pay a small fortune to a carpenter or plumber, because I'll be here to do more than is expected during the day-to-day routine of the job."

Can't you see the excitement on that employer's face? Out of twenty applicants for one job, that person's sure to stand out.

Perhaps you have no mechanical talents, but I would still encourage you to develop your teens' appreciation for appliances, tools, and so on by having them become a part of the solution when it comes to fixing something. They may learn that they have more skills than they dreamed of.

PUSH, BUT NOT TOO HARD.   How many parents have received a letter such as this one:

> Dear mom and dad:
> I've been in college for almost nine weeks, and boy am I lost! It's hard enough living on my own in the dorm, but I seem so far behind everyone else.

I wish you'd forced me to use the washer and dryer at home, because I wrecked my new sweater when I left it in the dryer too long. Since I never went food shopping, I didn't know that $20.00 buys almost nothing. Although I don't like to admit it, the first few times I went on the bus, I felt scared to death. I didn't know where it went or how to ask without looking stupid. All the other students seem to take care of themselves better than I do, but I'm learning fast.

In a way I'm mad I never learned all these things at home, but I also realize you did all those things for me out of love. If I'd been expected to do more around the house, maybe I would have appreciated all you did while I was still home.

Please force little Tommy to do more and be a part of the everyday running of the family as he grows up. I wouldn't want anyone to have to learn from 10,000 strangers, the way I've had to.

> Your number-one son,
> Bob

Parents who have taken care of their teens in this fashion can almost expect to receive a letter like this one day (though many teens might not feel they could say such things to them). Responsibility and handling life go hand in hand. When young people have not had responsibility placed in their hands—even *forced* into them—they have no resources with which to face the adult world.

Maturing is like climbing a set of stairs: You have to take one step to prepare for the next. As your teen develops in one area, he or she is ready to move on to a second. Many young people have not benefited from this stair exercise. They've spent so much time on fast-moving escalators that they're now out of shape.

When I suggest that you force your teen to take on responsibility, I'm not suggesting that you try to control her life, tell him what field to go into, or push her to exhaustion in the hobbies and sports she excels in. Every year many teens commit suicide because they feel they cannot live up to their parents' dreams for them. Or your young superstar may turn into a brat if you push him too far too fast.

My friend Fred told me how much it impressed him that his dad never forced him into becoming a farmer, too. Though his dad probably would have felt proud to have his son do so, he never stood in Fred's way when he chose another line of work.

Don't let anything like achievement ruin the relationship you have with your child. Keep the doors open. Some teens have shared with me that their parents won't even talk to them if they get less than the best grades or fail to run the fastest time. That's not fair to you or your child. It can destroy love in record time.

We have to find a middle ground between push, push, push and doing everything for our teens. Americans have a hard time not overdoing things: We put too much salt in our food; we chug our drinks, instead of sipping them; we drive too fast or too slow; we go all out on an exercise program for two weeks, then do nothing for two years. Don't overdo in either direction in raising your children.

Find the happy medium that will suit your child. Laziness seems to be America's national pastime, and we should not fall for that; but at the same time, we should never sacrifice our teens for our own unachieved goals. Study the long-term benefits for your child and look at your son or daughter's needs and desires. Then make a wise decision that will include as many angles as possible.

Sixteen

Give Them Resources with Which to Handle Life

W hen it comes to times of trouble, your teens need to know where to turn for help; and I hope you, mom and dad, are one of the strongest resources in your son or daughter's life. If you have bridged gaps between you so they can come to you on a regular basis, your young people will find they *can* handle difficult situations. But they also need to have some other alternatives, too. Let's look at all the resources.

GOD AND FAITH IN HIM.   The first person we should turn to in time of need is God. Since He created us, put us here, and knows more about each of us than anyone else, we should naturally ask Him for help in distress. By having a relationship with Him, we can receive guidance about every situation—what to do or what to stay away from. When we ask ourselves, *Have others encoun-*

tered this kind of problem? Or, *How desperate is this situation? What do I do now?* we can find the answers.

One girl shared this testimony of how her father influenced her family to build their faith in Jesus Christ:

"I remember our father would never let us leave the dinner table after our evening meal until we had a short Bible study. Sometimes they only lasted five or ten minutes, but usually twelve to fifteen minutes at the most. No matter how many kids were waiting at the door or what activity we needed to rush off to, we stayed at the table while we had a short Bible lesson. He would read, or we would read. Then we would briefly discuss it.

"There were days when each one would have a turn to prepare a short lesson, and we knew for at least twelve or fifteen minutes that evening we would have the entire family's undivided attention. We thought about it during the day. It was very special to know that people were going to listen to us give the lesson and give advice as to how to apply it.

"I can remember several times when we invited the neighbor kids in as they were waiting for us to come out and play. They so enjoyed our after-dinner Bible lessons that for a while we had to cut them off, because my father wanted it to be a special family time.

"As I look back over all the wonderful things that my parents did for all of us kids, I especially appreciate that special ritual, which was so meaningful to each one of us. It has taught me how to look into God's Word when I'm concerned, worried, alone, or afraid. It has also taught me that to be truly close and dear to someone, like God, it must be an everyday thought and action.

"I didn't always like those Bible studies. Many times I would close my ears, pretend not to listen, try hard not to concentrate, but it seemed the message came through. My entire life was touched, thanks to the little times at the end of our meals, which have shaped me in such a big way."

MOM AND DAD.   The second resource should be parents. Teens need confidence in mom and dad to come to you and benefit from your years of experience. Don't let your teens continually reinvent the wheel, because they do not have a chance to share your knowledge.

If they trust you, your son and daughter will ask questions like, "What would you do if . . ." "Have you ever felt as if . . ." "Is it normal to feel this way?" and so on.

Encourage your teens to talk, tell you what they think, and explain the situation. If you judge too hastily, your child may repeat the mournful words of one teen, who told me: "I wish my parents would treat me as a friend instead of a son or daughter. They seem to give their opinions too quickly, never listen, and continually say things like, 'Why do you always,' or, 'You should do this or that.' I know that they don't talk to their friends like this. Why should I be any different from a true friend?"

Instead of alienating your young people by jumping to a conclusion, why not listen, then advise, gently and carefully, sharing the lessons you've learned through your own bruises, hurts, and tears.

THEMSELVES.   Teens should learn to look inside themselves and have confidence in their own ability to reason, to decide what is right and wrong, to follow their intuition. Encourage your son or daughter to think, *I'm a person. I've handled difficult things before. How should I deal with this?* Teach your teens to look inside themselves when they make a decision—help them make it a lifetime habit. It's something they'll need to work over and over again as they say no to drugs or premarital sex and yes to the right things in life.

CHURCH PEOPLE.   A fourth resource should be the church community—your pastor, elders, or members with whom they have a close relationship. Encourage your teens to talk to others who belong to your church and to learn from their experiences of faith. Many Christians have exciting stories they'd be happy to share.

Every young person needs some outside adults to go to at times. Your church is a good place to find responsible people who share your beliefs and can help your teen grow spiritually.

FAMILY AND NEIGHBORS.   This could include grandparents, an aunt or uncle, or wise neighbors—people who can have a powerful good impact on your teen.

Time and time again, young people tell me they receive encouragement from their immediate families and no one else. Everyone needs feedback from people outside the home—it builds confidence. So encourage another family member, a close friend, or a neighbor to talk to your son or daughter. Remember, the parent who becomes jealous of such friendships hinders the self-respect of his or her teen. Instead, become that kind of friend to another young person you know.

As a benefit from such encouragement, teens may also develop an ability to care for others. Don't let your child avoid people of different ages or types. One teen whose parents brought her to visit her grandmother learned a great lesson:

"As I grew up, we always paid special attention to my grandparents. When my grandmother went into the nursing home, we as a family would visit her and other people that we didn't even know. It was very awkward and scary being around people who don't move or talk much. Many of them lay on the beds, motionless, some were in wheelchairs, and others seemed to sleep all the time. But I learned that *people need people,* and just because someone is old does not mean that he is useless or worthless.

"My parents taught me to ask my grandmother, in her later years, questions about life and how to live it. I asked her what she remembered and, 'Were they really the "good ol' days?" ' It is very easy now for me to talk to a person of any age, old or young. I'm not afraid of old people, and I'm not afraid of babies, largely because my parents took me and somewhat forced me to meet them and interact with them.

"I will always be grateful for this part of my childhood. My parents took something that most kids my age were definitely afraid of and helped me become a better person by making me become familiar with it."

FRIENDS.   Another resource should be other well-respected friends who have proven themselves and handled situations well. Teach your teen to look for individuals who care about their safety and future, who have enough courage to say no when they have to. Help your son or daughter to chose the right friends— people who will help them grow personally, emotionally, physically, and spiritually. Friends can build a teen up or tear him down.

Ask your teens, "What has the crowd you hang around with gained from you in the last month?" Then ask, "What have you gained from them?" Quite often you will notice that a person takes on the traits of a crowd. Are there actions, activities or habits your teen has started to do because of the crowd? What virtues, morals, habits, and so on does that group call cool?

When your teens clearly look at those questions, quite often they realize the group has gained nothing from them, but they have, chameleonlike, taken on the traits of the group. Then they may realize they don't want to follow their friends down every path.

Ask them valuable questions such as, "What have you started doing because of them? What have they started doing because of you?"

How about those special people your teen dates? When it came to boyfriends, one young woman explained her parents' attitudes:

"My father wouldn't let me date any boy unless he met him over dinner. Sometimes it was the most nerve-racking experience ever seen, but usually it turned out for the best. My father wanted to look each and every guy over very carefully before he allowed him to take me out on a date.

"I was seventeen years old, and I used to get very angry at him because none of my friends did anything like this. I probably didn't have nearly as many dates as any of the other girls, either. But the dates that I did have were fun and enjoyable, and I never got taken advantage of (probably they figured my dad would be waiting to talk with them at the end of the evening, as well! Of course, he didn't).

"As I look back on this situation my dad placed on me, I'm very thankful for it. Though I didn't agree with or enjoy it at the time, I now see how many young people get into trouble by going wherever and whenever they please. In a way, my father showed his love by going the extra mile and spending the extra time with me.

"When I have teenagers of my own, I'm going to insist on the same old-fashioned policy."

Be certain you know something of the young people your son or daughter dates. Make them welcome in your home, because then you have a greater opportunity to help your child and know his or her friends.

In addition to these friends, encourage your teen to have the resources of a teacher, principal, or guidance counselor at school. Perhaps an older brother or sister could also double as a friend.

Every person has many resources available. Help your teens become aware of the people who could help in a difficult situation. Teach them to turn to those who have knowledge and experience in such areas.

Seventeen

Help Them Find Heroes

When I pick up a newspaper or magazine and read about a poll testing who today's teens have as their current heroes, I often go away feeling appalled. Their favorites change like the wind, but worse, they so often seem to be people who have few really admirable characteristics: Quite often they have no moral foundation or family structure; maybe they use drugs—and are proud of it. The teens who admire such heroes have based that opinion on the fleeting moments of popularity that have brought a Hollywood leading man, music superstar, or sports figure to the world's attention.

When I see a student who admires his dad most of all, because he has seen what his father stands for, through his life-style and beliefs, I feel more hopeful for our teens. If a student tells me he admires his pastor or Jesus Christ or a famous person with a well-rounded life, I feel encouraged.

Give Your Teen a Hero

Every teen needs someone to look up to, and like most parents, you'd probably like your son or daughter to admire a person who shares the values you've tried to teach. To make certain this happens, give your young person a hand in finding people who have those good traits you'd like to see developed in his or her life.

One way to do that is to encourage your teen to read biographies of famous people. As she reads, help her understand that a person can be famous and not have life all together. Help him take a critical look at a man or woman's life-style to see what he can learn from it. From the stories of some achievers, your son can learn the value of keeping the family together and happy, while the business grows; your daughter can learn the importance of keeping integrity intact, while making money. Help them learn from the mistakes and experiences of others. By seeing that another person has had deep problems and has overcome them; by learning that you can fail at one job and succeed in another; by understanding that a person can become unpopular for something, without facing the end of the world; by knowing that people made fun of a great man, your teen can see more of life's realities. From such stories he or she may gain courage.

Let your teens know that some heroes may not last long, that some people do lose faith and lose out. As I wrote this book, the newspapers splashed the story of Len Bias over their pages. The young basketball star seemed to have it all going for him. Right after being chosen second in the NBA player draft, by the world-champion Boston Celtics, he went out to celebrate his new career. Although Len Bias was known for his levelheadedness and straight life-style, cocaine caused his death. According to the doctors, the 100 percent pure drug caused his brain to malfunction, and he had convulsions and died within minutes. We may never know the truth of that young man's death, but many suffered the tragedy of it. When you hear of such situations, share with your teens. Let them know that one mistake may be a final one—and encourage them to make wise decisions the first time.

For both good and bad examples, turn to the Bible. There you can find stories of heroes who made it in one area, but not another, and you can discover stories of admirable people, too. Encourage your teens to read God's Word on their own and understand the impact one life can have on another.

As they look for people to admire and follow in life, guide your teens. In your own life, act in ways they can look up to. One day you may feel the happiness of knowing your son or daughter would like to become just like you! Even if you don't become a hero, have the comfort of knowing your teen has good ones, who stand for important values—help your child discern the good points of the people he or she looks up to.

Eighteen

Train Them to Make Good Decisions

A friend of mine once compared the brain to a car—both have two places that hold things. The front of the brain holds short-term messages and is like the glove compartment. The back of the brain holds the long-term stuff—just like the trunk of a car.

When we hear messages once or twice, they go in our minds' glove compartments, but the long-term ones—the ones we really remember—go into the trunk if we program, rehearse, drill, and repeat them, using emotions to increase their power.

When you go on a trip, where do you put your luggage? In the glove compartment? No, you put it in the trunk. That's where some messages to our teens should be—and in order to get there, we have to repeat them over and over, until the truth goes to the back of the brain, where our young people won't forget it.

Many of the teens others call troublemakers, my friend Reggie

131

Smith says, have trouble making it with what the adults in their lives have given them to store in their trunks. He says they have nothing but "junk in their trunks."

What kind of luggage does your teen have in life? What can you do to improve it?

Junk in Your Trunk?

In order for teens to have successful lives, they need opportunities to learn how to make good choices. How can they do that if parents have never prepared them for the future by giving them important information that will help and a chance to try it out?

If you don't teach your child how to do this, someone else will and you may not like the results of their teaching. Not everyone will share your view of what's important or right.

One evening I stayed up to watch the "Tonight Show," hosted by Johnny Carson. As I tuned in, he was asking the audience, "What would you do if . . .?" Using the game "Scruples," he asked questions designed to reflect character and integrity. The way he and Ed McMahon handled this really showed me where most parents miss the boat when it comes to teaching young people life lessons.

Johnny and Ed asked: "If you were a mile from the grocery store, and you noticed your five-year-old son had taken a fifty-cent candy bar, what would you do?"

Together they reasoned, "Well, it's not worth the gas to go back. Should you take it next time, if you think of it? Or should you forget it, because you might have trouble explaining things? What would you do?" they asked the audience. They never came up with an answer.

That night millions of Americans were learning how to parent and handle tough situations from TV. Unfortunately, they weren't watching "Little House on the Prairie" or "The Cosby Show." Instead they got junk in their trunks.

I'd like to give you my suggestion about how you can handle the candy-bar situation. First you stop the car and discuss the problem with your son. Explain what stealing is. Say something like: "You know how you like your new tennis shoes. How would you feel if your friend Jimmy came over and took them home with him? You wouldn't like that, would you? You would feel sad and probably very angry.

"What should Jimmy do if he took them? That's right, bring them back. The grocery man feels the same way about his candy bar. Let's go make him happy by taking it back. Okay?" Then forget about the cost of the gas and drive back.

When you get to the store, go in with your son and help him explain it to the manager, but let the boy do most of the talking. Afterward praise him for his courage and character. Explain that he should never do that again, but that mom and dad will be there in any difficulty.

When you've done that with a child, you've accomplished two things:

> You've taught him a life lesson in honesty.
> You've reinforced the idea that you are in
>   this thing together.

Teach Life Lessons

I'd like to suggest that every teen needs to learn to put things in his or her trunk through two techniques:

> Seeing it in life situations.
> Hearing it from mom and dad.

Whatever we *tell* our teens, we may have taught them, but that may not be enough to make a real change in their life-style. If we want to have a real impact, we have to show them, as well as tell them. They see what we do as well as hear what we say.

Try these tips for teaching life lessons by reinforcing your words with your deeds:

WHEN YOU TALK TO YOUR TEEN, GIVE SPECIFICS.   The key to helping your child make a wise decision is to give specific facts that will help in the process. For example, if you need to talk with your son about sex, tell him, when he enters puberty, exactly what he can expect with the changes in his body, emotions, and social life. Give your daughter that information, too, adding specific lines guys may use in order to have sex with her. Share how she can say no.

With both son and daughter, reinforce the fact that the onetime, fun-filled activity of having sex could totally ruin a teen's life. A girl could have to deal with a pregnancy, before she's much more than a child herself. She might have to live with the consequences of an abortion. Both boy and girl could suffer from a divorce, venereal disease, a bad reputation, and low self-esteem.

Talking with your thirteen-year-old once and never mentioning sex again is practically useless, because you've only put it in the glove compartment. Be specific and reinforce the message often. Keep open communication channels, so you can continue providing information that can help in an embarrassing or difficult situation.

Imagine sixteen-year-old Mary with her boyfriend, Jim. It is late, they are alone, and he starts to apply pressure for her to have sex with him. She has no way home if she says no, so it seems easier to go along with him. She feels a real inner struggle with her conscience.

Mary knows she shouldn't be out this late alone, and her parents will get upset if she comes home late. But something her mom told her keeps coming back: "No matter how late or where you are, if you are in any type of trouble or being faced with something you don't want to do, call me anytime, and I'll come for you."

Because Mary's mother gave her this vital cargo, in the form of repeated words, she has the courage to say no and ask to be taken home. She knows that if her boyfriend gives her trouble, she can call mom. In the past she has had the freedom to stand up for her rights; now she makes use of it. Jim goes along with her, and his respect for her grows greatly.

When she gets home, Mary shares with her mom and thanks her for always being there. Their relationship grows stronger, and Mary gains strength in standing up for herself.

As Mary described what happened, her mother didn't blame or condemn her; instead she congratulated Mary on a good decision. The fact that her mother listened and didn't get angry reconfirmed to Mary that she really wanted to talk things over. Because this wise parent has "walked what she talked," her daughter has bought the message, and she has given Mary a valuable resource to turn to when sixteen years of experience aren't enough.

Don't pass by what I call the "daily disasters," however small. You can't afford to. *Train* your teen, don't *teach* him. You can teach a child by saying, "You shouldn't steal because it's wrong." Say it once, and you have taught a lesson, but training means you make it stick by showing how it applies. Look for the opportunities to show him real-life truths: how well honest people sleep at night and how proud their families feel of them; how people in prisons weren't honest with themselves or others. My Bible says, *"Train* up a child in the way he should go; and when he is old, he will not depart from it" (*italics mine*). Make use of that parenting truth.

REMEMBER WHAT IT'S LIKE TO BE A TEEN.   Another way to improve communication with your teen and help build success in decision making is to remember and share specifics about your teen years. Your son won't feel quite so devastated if he knows that you didn't make the team, either, when you were in high school (assuming you can convince him you *had* sports way back then!).

To help you in this, I've provided a set of questions to share with your son or daughter. Fill it out, adding any others you may find appropriate.

1. What do you remember most when you were growing up?
2. What did your parents do that you really appreciated?
3. What did your parents do that made you mad or angry?
4. Who was your best friend?
5. What types of activities did you do for fun?
6. Was it hard or easy to learn to drive a car?
7. Did you like sports?
8. What extracurricular activities did you enjoy?
9. How did you feel about God, church, Sunday school, the Bible, your pastor?
10. Who were your heroes? Why?
11. What grades did you get in math, English, and so on?
12. Did you ever flunk a class?
13. What did you fear the most as a teen?

14. What dreams did you have that came true? Never came true?
15. Who believed in you the most?
16. Who could you talk to about anything?
17. What was your greatest disappointment growing up? Greatest joy? Greatest sorrow?
18. When was the first time you tried smoking, drinking, or sex? How did you struggle with it? Were you happy or mad at yourself for trying?
19. How was technology different then?
20. How old are you? In comparison with the rest of your teen's friends' parents?
21. What do you most regret doing?
22. What do you wish you had done?
23. Did you have to earn your own money? How? Did you like it at the time? As you look back are you glad you had the opportunity?
24. How did you feel about the elderly?
25. Were you popular in school? Why? Why not?
26. Where did you go on dates? What did you do?
27. Were your parents too strict? Too lenient?
28. Did you ever lie or steal? How did you handle it? How did you feel about it?
29. Were you ever depressed? About what? How did you handle it?

When you share with your teen, use discretion, but don't make that a reason to cop out, either. On some moral issues, it may seem wiser to hold back a bit. (To that a teen might say, "Yeah, that's what I thought. They never share about sex. How can I learn, except on my own?") I'm not advising you to ignore the topic, instead share generalities in such places.

In most areas you'll want to share specifics. Teens need to know how you felt about girls (or boys), and whether or not you went to the senior prom. Give them a nucleus of information, so you can show how normal you were and are.

As you share with your teen, you give him the information he needs to have a successful future. You help her make the hard decisions that will lead to good choices for tomorrow. Help your son and daughter put positive messages in their trunks. It could become one of the most important life lessons you give.

Nineteen

Teens Need Their Parents to ...

Train Them to Confide

When I speak to parents, I often hear the question, "How do I get my son [or daughter] to come to me when he [or she] is in trouble?" My head spins from the number of times I hear, "My teens never come to me.. Why don't they trust me? I tell them to come to me, but they never do. Can you explain it?"

I really think I do have an answer for the parents who ask those questions. Even though you may have told your son and daughter a thousand times that they should come to you in trouble, it's still only sitting in the glove compartment and hasn't made it to the trunk yet.

Training a teen to confide in you compares to teaching a child basic math. If you tell your six-year-old daughter, "Two plus two equals four," and write it ten times: $2 + 2 = 4$, the idea won't sink in. Why? She's still only put it in the glove compartment. Only by seeing it over and over again, by studying math all year in school and seeing lots of problems where $2 + 2 = 4$, will it move into her trunk. After a year, you won't have to mention it again. She'll understand the concept for life.

In the same way, you have to work on your teen's perception to help him understand that he can come to you in trouble. Look for day-to-day situations that will store that message in your child's trunk.

Here are some specific steps you can take, to carry out that plan.

NEVER TALK DOWN TO YOUR TEEN.   Instead of acting as if he can't understand what you're talking about or becoming impatient with him, try to find out what your son means by his statements. Attempt to find out what's going on in your daughter's mind when she says, "Everything is okay. There's nothing wrong, really. I'm doing fine," but other signals she gives don't agree. Realize that few times in a teen's life will she have everything okay and nothing to trouble her.

When your teen uses the "everything is okay" line, it usually means she wants you to persist a little more and show that you really care about her. Keep asking. Don't question her in a testy way, but in a caring, "I love you" way that will make her want to open up and share what's on her mind.

THINK BEFORE YOU SPEAK.   Before you talk to your son as if he were a forty-year-old, remember what it felt like to be a teen.

When you walk in your son's room and say, "How can you live in a room like that?" you've shown him you've forgotten how easy it is for a teen to live in messed-up space. Deep inside, your son knows a messy bedroom's just a temporary stop between here and eternity. He also knows that neighbors don't really peek in on him and think, *She's a bad mother. Just look at that boy's room.* So don't sweat it.

Dad, if you find your daughter's shoes in the hall, don't ask, "Who left these shoes out here?" It's obvious to her you don't know what's going on! Your daughter owns the shoes—and she probably left them there. By making such comments you blow off steam, but you don't train your teen to put her shoes away.

Avoid other statements such as:

"How many times do I have to tell you . . .?"
"I hope you have ten kids just like you when you grow up."
"When I was your age. . . ."
"Can't you ever . . .?"
"How many times will you . . .?"

When you use such phrases, you expect your teen to look at life through an adult's eyes. Remember that your child doesn't have the experience you do and needs time to develop in many areas.

Use some common sense when you talk to your teens. Let them know, by your words, that you really do care what they think and feel.

LET YOUR TEENS DO THINGS FOR YOU.   Don't do everything for your young people. Suppose something in your son's room needs fixing. If he could fix it, follow these simple rules:

1. Tell him how to do it.
2. If you must, walk him through the project, but don't make it sound as if he'll be incompetent.
3. Let him goof up, if necessary.
4. If he breaks something, that's all right. The process of his learning to be independent and handle things on his own is much more important than a broken piece of glass or spilled milk.

5. Show him you believe in his ability to work through problems.
6. If he asks for help, give him advice. Don't do it for him. If you must show him, *only* show him. Let him do it on his own.
7. Ask questions like, "What will you need for this project?" "When will you need to start in order to finish painting the porch in time to go on your hiking trip?" Let him realize that he needs to begin thinking for himself and working through these situations. Unless you teach him how to think ahead, he may never learn it. Teach him how to cover all the bases, so a project will turn out right.

WHEN YOUR TEEN GOOFS UP, DON'T TELL HER WHAT HAP-PENED AND HOW TO FIX IT.   Instead, ask her what she saw in her mind, how it happened, and how *she* feels she should fix it. This way she will learn to work through problems by herself.

When you do this, you begin to train your teen how to look at her resources, when a problem arises, and how to make the good decisions that will help her say no to the things she doesn't believe in and say yes to the things she wants in her life.

Give her the reasons and the how-tos (luggage in her trunk), to say yes to tomorrow's possibilities and the normality of today's problems.

AVOID STATEMENTS THAT SHOW A LACK OF BELIEF IN YOUR CHILD'S ABILITY TO DO THINGS ON HIS OWN.   This includes such comments as:

"Do it just like this. . . ."
"Don't forget to do that."
"Please remember what I told you last week."

Instead show him you have belief in his abilities by saying sentences like:

> "You can handle it."
> "John, I really need your help. . . ."
> "Could you give me a hand with this?"
> "We've got a problem out there. Could you go handle it?"

By saying such things, you reinforce your teen's belief that you have faith in his competence. He may come to you with questions, and that is the time to share with him. When he asks, help him handle whatever comes up. You've given him the encouragement he needs.

AFTER AN ACTIVITY, DISCUSS WHAT HAPPENED AND HOW YOUR TEEN FELT.   When your daughter comes home from youth group, a class at school that she doesn't like, when she feels mad at someone, or when she's made the cheerleading squad, talk about what happened. Ask what made her feel good or bad; listen to her, on her own terms.

By opening your ears and eyes and closing your mouth, you can find out more about your children. Let them share what went right and wrong in a project or experience, what they can do to make it happen again or not happen again. As they have a chance to share their hurts and joys, showing emotions about what has happened, they will grow and develop their ability to handle problems.

Have your son analyze why certain teens in school always get in trouble. Is it the authorities' fault or that of the students? Have your daughter share why she likes or dislikes a certain teacher, why she thought a speaker was boring or interesting. Ask what she would do differently in these cases. What would she copy?

Talk through your own reasons for certain things, too. Give your teens vital information about why you think the way you do, so that they will understand why you act the way you do.

TAKE YOUR TEEN SERIOUSLY.   Ask your son's advice in a situation. If he gives you some, follow through on it, if possible. Show him you take him seriously. Many young people think of themselves as dumb kids because no one has ever let them prove themselves. Because mom and dad give them this message, they don't expect the rest of the world to take them seriously, either.

Once you've followed up on his advice, let your son know how it worked and how much you appreciate his suggestion. Tell him that what he thinks and knows are important. Your positive opinion's crucial to his growth.

LOG THE TIME YOU SPEND WITH EACH FAMILY MEMBER.   For one week, write down the activity, discussion, experience, or project you worked on, then put the person's name and the amount of time you spent together. By becoming aware of your habits and making changes in them, you can grow closer to each member and raise the number of hours you truly communicate with your family.

As you figure this, do not count time spent watching TV. Sitting shoulder to shoulder, looking at a television screen, doesn't bring you nearer to understanding your teen or spouse. Discussing a program, letting each person in the family have a say *is* time well spent.

It takes many hours to become close to your teen—and quite a bit of effort. Because they have so many activities and busy schedules, sometimes you'll find it hard to get together.

Make the log a priority, and you'll see the truth in the national PTA's statistic that parents spend an average of less than fourteen minutes a week with their teens. You may also understand why they say parents use twelve of those fourteen minutes giving directions: "Come home on time." "Don't forget to. . . ." "Make sure you don't. . . ." Only two or three minutes a week were spent really communicating! What happened to the time that should have been spent discussing ideas, sharing feelings, talking over problems, asking questions, sharing a laugh, hurting together, praying with each other? Try to develop those in your lives.

DISCUSS WITH YOUR CHILD WHAT HER STRONG POINTS ARE. Sit down with your teen, take a sheet of paper, and write down some of her good points (see "Family Test," in chapter 3). Then share them with her. Quite often you can think of strengths she never knew she had. Perhaps you can ask some of her friends to testify to them. Help her realize her good points, and show her that she has some you don't. Point out that you ask her advice in some areas where she's better than you. Show her how proud you feel of the areas in which she's worked and made herself strong.

But be careful that you don't try to build her up to develop areas where she has no talent or natural gifts. Don't praise another child's ability in field hockey if your daughter's naturally clumsy or comment on how pretty a friend is if she could never compete in that area. Instead choose things you know she excels in or could become good in. If you must, approve of and brag on someone else's child (only in an area she could develop in). Tell her how much you thought of Cindy, who memorized the most Bible verses in the Sunday-school class, or talk about Dan, who kept up a neighbor's yard while she was in the hospital. When you mention these things, your daughter may feel she has to grow and live up to someone else's good deeds. She *can* reach for and accomplish them.

Take another sheet and discuss her interests. Show her they go hand in hand with her abilities. Maybe she'll realize why she does better in some classes than others. Get her thinking about what kind of career, profession, or summer job she might like to try—one that would make the most use of her abilities.

MAKE A LIST OF YOUR CHILD'S WEAKNESSES.   After you've looked at her strong points, gently show your daughter her weak ones. As you develop a list of areas in which you think she could improve, also list some of your own weak points, to take the sting out of the exercise. Let her know that everyone has weaknesses and things they can work on. We all need improving somewhere.

If you can see something (with your thirty or forty years' experience) that will hurt her communication, tell her so in a tactful way and encourage her to work on it. If your daughter tends to brag, don't say, "Don't you know that when you talk that way, the other kids will ignore you? Can't you see that it alienates you from other students?" She *doesn't* know; no one has ever taught her. So take this opportunity to do so. You have a great opportunity to mold her and help her become the kind of woman you can be proud of.

At the same time share stories of how you have overcome weaknesses and made them into strengths. Even better, mention some famous personalities who have done that. Do some reading, if you have to, to find some current people who have changed significantly.

MAKE A LIST OF YOUR TEEN'S FEARS.   Sit down with your son and make a list of his fears. What is he afraid of? Why? What scares him most? What does he worry about? Why?

Next to the list, answer the question, "Can we do something about this, or is it out of our hands?" If you can find a solution, do. If not, at least you will not have to spend as much time dealing with it. Why worry about something you can't change?

Become one of the rare parents who has done this with a teen. It's so unusual that your child may share with others the importance of the time you've spent together, and he will certainly know you feel committed to his well-being.

FIND OUT WHAT YOUR CHILD DOES FOR OTHERS.   Actually, for this you'll make two lists. The first will describe the things you do for your teen. Include everything you do automatically for him, especially ones you don't say anything about. Chances are that when you finish the list, you'll discover some things he should do for himself. Then you need to ask him to take on those responsibilities.

Next make a list of things your teen should do for others; when prompted, does for others; and just goes ahead and does for them. Congratulate him on what he already does and encourage him to develop new areas of service.

One of the best ways of letting a person grow is to let him do things for you. When you do too much for a teen, it may harm him by keeping him from taking on responsibility he needs. Show him the benefits of serving—for himself and others.

Don't limit your son's help to you, either. Point out how he can help the neighbors, take food to the homeless, make a gift for an orphan child, write a letter to missionaries, pick up a paper he didn't drop, look for frowns to turn upside down, and help around the house (without getting paid for it).

As your teens realize that what they do for others really builds character and shows them they have the ability to be givers, not just takers, they will grow in a way you've never seen before. Give them practice in this area.

COME UP WITH A NEW ACTIVITY AROUND THE HOUSE.   Each week, try to find something new to do with your children. Maybe you've always mown the lawn by yourself. Invite your son or daughter to help. Watch what happens when you work side by side. New friendships will develop and old ones will grow.

Try including a few of these activities in your plans:

Paint a room together
Wash the car
Read a book
Go to the dump
Work in the garden
Move furniture around
Organize a bookshelf
Memorize Scripture
Cook
Balance the checkbook
Decide on a family vacation
Build a doghouse
Visit a nursing home
Work at church
Rake leaves

Add to that list with your own ideas, but try to make certain you do something at least once a week. As you work together, communication between you and your teen will become natural. You'll grow closer to your child than you ever dreamed possible. You'll also become a part of your child's difficult teen years.

What cherished memories do you have of your parents? They were times spent with you, weren't they? Because we all spend time in areas and activities we enjoy, the fact that mom and dad spent time with you showed they loved you. It's no different with your teens: You'll need to give them time if you want to show them you love them.

If spending time with your teen is a new habit, don't wait for it to *feel* fun before you start. Instead, start spending the time together, and the emotion will follow. Psychologists can tell you it's easier to act yourself into feelings than to feel yourself into actions!

DON'T TURN TRADITIONS INTO HANDCUFFS.   Make a list of the traditions in your family; then ask your teen to help come up with new ones and analyze old ones to discover why they're important to her. Find out which ones you need to give more leeway on and which you need to have happen more regularly.

One young man shared a tradition his girl friend, Jane, had in her home. Her family believed in God, His Son, and His Word. At a very young age her parents encouraged her to become active in the church and to go there regularly. Jane had accepted Christ as her Savior and felt excited about her faith. They had given her a fine tradition.

But now that she's in her twenties and lives at home, Jane's parents demand such rigid attendance that she's begun to grow cold toward her church. She would love to check out a few other churches, to see what they are like and compare them to her own, but her parents won't allow it.

It seems to me that Jane needs to experience things for herself and decide how real and viable a faith she has. Without the firsthand experience of how God can and will help her in trials and joys, without some personal experiences, that wonderful tradition could turn into alienation.

If her parents have equipped her to handle life with God as her best friend, I wonder what they feel worried about. Why not let Jane go and explore with Him? Isn't He big enough to speak to her heart, if she leaves their church? Didn't they teach her to have discernment? What do they fear?

In another tradition—the family vacation—you might want to meet your teens halfway. Your children might want to take along a friend. Unless that's totally out of the question, it might be the best thing you can do. Show your teens that you take them for real, and let them bring someone with them.

On the other side of the coin, many traditions that may seem small and meaningless to you may mean the world to your teens. A small thing like knowing certain things happened last Christmas and will happen next year can add stability and a sense of security to their lives. Ask what ones your teens most enjoy and develop them into a regular part of your lives.

Your family will take the cue from you, so discover which traditions they find special. Ask how communication between you could improve. Most of the time, your teens will tell you!

ENCOURAGE FAMILY CONFERENCES.   Whenever a problem arises in your family, make it possible for anyone to call a conference. Don't talk it over at mealtime, instead agree upon a special time when no distractions will occur. Turn off the TV, unplug the phone, and set aside a good amount of time for discussion. Allow everyone a fair say, without being jumped on or shouted at. Keep everything at normal voice level.

By using this technique, you will show your teens how to discuss difficulties and problems with others. You'll also give your children the same common courtesy you allow a co-worker or teammate whose opinion differs from yours.

Teens want to hear things in a grown-up way and this activity can help them do that. But if you come down to a final decision and have no firm ground for it, mom and dad must have the final say. When your teens come to you often for conferences, you probably won't have much trouble like this. After all, they feel comfortable enough with you to talk things out. (They'll have to have experienced some of the other things we've already considered before they'll ask for a family conference in the first place.)

Once you've developed a good communication system with your teens, keep it open with the family conference.

PRACTICE WRITTEN DIALOGUE.   I'd encourage you to make this meaningful exercise a part of your communication. You and your teen each get out a sheet of paper. Decide on a topic: It might be "What I admire most about you." Go into separate rooms for fifteen minutes and write all you can on the topic. At the end of that time, come back into the same room, take a few minutes to read each other's notes on the subject, then discuss them for ten minutes more. You'll find you've written many things you've always wanted to say, but have never had a chance to.

As you write, don't wander from the topic or use the word *but*. Include the positive and negative things. Share in a friendly, mature manner the areas in which you wish the other would act differently, but give your feedback *only* in a positive fashion.

As you do this exercise with your teen, you'll teach him how to put feelings on paper, to admit that he can love or be angry with someone, and realize that feelings count.

MAKE IT EASY FOR YOUR TEEN TO DO HOMEWORK.   Give your son time and a quiet place to do work in. Don't structure too many activities that take a lot of time on a night when you know he has a lot of work. As they arise, help your teen accomplish projects. Sit down and learn a subject with him. Read a memory book along with him, and teach him some memory skills he can use for homework.

Although many students don't need more homework, they need a home to do it in. Become considerate of the time your teens have to spend on it. Encourage them to take that time and do the work. By doing this they will learn responsibility and self-control. When your daughter works hard to raise a D to a C, give her appreciation, even though she didn't make an A. Notice improvement and comment on it. As you do, your teens will learn to do the same thing for their children someday.

HELP YOUR TEENS ASSUME RESPONSIBILITY AND FULL CONTROL OF THEIR LIVES.   Here are some ideas that can get you started.

1. Make sure your son starts taking control of himself. To make it happen, change your family's life-style if you have to.

2. Teach your daughter to focus on the fact that even though television teaches us that life has instant solutions, it doesn't. Help her realize that even though the typical sitcom shows a problem at 8:00, followed by a solution by 8:30, life doesn't work that way.

    Also show her that advertising that implies a product will make her sexy, beautiful, successful, or rich aims to sell something, not to tell the truth. Help her know that nothing she buys can end obstacles, put-downs, or frustrations in her life.

3. Don't manipulate events and activities so that your child looks like a winner. When you do this, you prove to your son or daughter that he or she *can't* handle things alone. Bruises and tears hurt, but they also often allow a child to turn to God, seek inner strength and solutions, and to come to you and other resource people.

4. When your child says, "Do this for me," "Please handle that for me," "Fix this for me," encourage him or her to do it alone. Get your son in the habit of doing his own laundry and your daughter competent in handling sim-

ple tools. If you baby-sit a teen in high school, he'll expect it in college. If you continually pick up the pieces each time your daughter falls to the ground, when she's twenty-five or thirty, she'll wonder why society doesn't do it for her.

5. When you deal with your child's teacher, develop the attitude "let's work this out together with my child. Help me reach her. Help me help you with your situation at school." Don't go to the school expecting its staff to do everything and demanding it all for your child. If a teacher makes a stand, look at both sides, and (most often) take the side of the teacher. I know in some cases you will have to take the part of your child, but remember that thirty years ago, when parents stood behind teachers, schools had very little rebellion and few discipline problems. When one independent study asked high-school seniors what else they wished their teachers had done for them, these young men and women answered: (1) love them more, (2) expect more out of them, and (3) been tougher on them.

6. Teach your children to pray about answers and solutions to problems. Teach them to look to God for guidance, while walking through life's trials, searching for the best way to handle a problem. Rather than letting teens just leave a trouble in God's lap, encourage them to keep moving while they wait for the response from God—He directs moving feet. The Bible may not include Ben Franklin's saying, "God helps them that help themselves," but many times it works that way.

Help your teens realize they need to control their actions. Each day they choose what to do, say, when to work or to play, and who to do it with.

Use these and other techniques to help your teen become a self-confident, independent adult, and you will have done a fine job of parenting.

Where Do You Go From Here?

Good parenting takes much time, patience, and effort. Once you've conceived and borne a child, you can't just leave off there. Nor can you trade in your teen for another model, even on your most frustrating days.

Use the techniques I've provided here to help build a better relationship with your son or daughter. Make the most of the ideas that seem to fit your family's needs and try some new steps that can give your life some zing. Though you may not find any easy answers, you could find some powerful ones.

As you begin to find out more about your teens, they'll begin telling you more of the things they've always wanted you to know but were afraid to tell you. (By then you probably won't need to look back at this book too often. You might even decide to write your own!)

If you would like to share any questions, problems, or answers with me, please drop me a note at:

> Bill Sanders
> P.O. Box 711
> Portage, MI 49081

Appendix:
Commitment Contract between Parent and Teen

As you encourage your teen to take responsibility for his or her own life you may want to make a contract together.

Initially that may seem a bit frightening, because people see images of money, lawyers, and big deals, when they think about contracts. But you can use one effectively in the family, too, for any child above the age of seven. (The younger the child, the simpler you need to keep a contract, though.)

A contract states a written goal you and your child intend to fulfill. You don't just *wish* or *hope to* keep it, you *will* keep to the agreement.

Using a contract has many purposes:

1. It puts the rules down on paper, so you both know what to expect of each other.
2. It leaves little room for misunderstanding, later on.
3. It gives each person a greater commitment to live up to the contract.
4. It eliminates excuses for not going through with your part of the contract. Teens really seem to respect contracts, because they feel their parents have treated them as adults.

When a parent and teen use a contract, they make life more fulfilling by working together as a team. Each person commits himself to the other's needs and feelings, as well as his own.

You may want to use a contract for these purposes:

1. *Communication*. You may wish to state that your teen can call you on the phone anytime, from anywhere, and you will come get him or her. Or you may make a contract that says your young people may call a family conference at any time.

   A contract like this is a two-way street. Whatever privilege you give to one, the other also has.
2. *Drug abuse*. You may agree with your teen to have a contract that he or she will stay away from drugs throughout the high-

155

school years. As parents, you, too, will have to agree to stay away from any drugs you use (alcohol, Valium, or cigarettes). Although you may reason it's perfectly legal for you to use alcohol or prescribed drugs, your child looks up to you as a role model. Realize that you must "show and tell."

3. *Household responsibilities.* Make an agreement concerning chores, allowances, privileges, phone use, homework, and so on. This way everyone will know what is expected and can act accordingly.

4. *Friendships and dating.* You may wish to state when you will allow your daughter to date, how often she may go out, and how late she may stay out. In return you may want her to have you meet her date, give him permission to date her, know where they are going and how late they expect to be.

5. *Use of the car.* Have an understanding of how and when your teen needs to check the oil or take care of other maintenance, who will pay the insurance (and when), how car payments will be made.

Young people usually can live up to the heights their parents show them. Although they may meet and exceed the expectations of their parents, more often, what they can't see, they never reach. When we give them clear-cut, well-defined, and reasonable expectations, they strive for them. A contract is simply one method of doing this.

Talk to your teen about setting up a contract. You may be surprised at how well he or she receives the idea. Then you can use one similar to the form below.

Parent: I commit to

Teen: I commit to

Signed: Parent
            Teen
            Date

Bill Sanders is the best-selling author of youth devotionals such as *Outtakes for Girls* and *Guys* and *Goalposts for Girls* and *Guys*. He speaks at high schools and other youth meetings across the country.